The CDO Journey

Insights and Advice Gleaned from Practicing Data Leaders

To: Mom + Dad
Cause you are
always there!
XOXO
Kath (see page 2)

Peter Aiken, Todd Harbour, Ed Kelly, Burt
Walsh, Kathy Walter

Foreword by Matthew Millea

Technics Publications

Published by:

2 Lindsley Road, Basking Ridge, NJ 07920 USA
https://www.TechnicsPub.com

Edited by Juanita Billings
Cover design by Hih7 Webtech Pvt Ltd.

First Printing 2020

Copyright © 2020 by Peter Aiken, Todd Harbour, Edward Kelly, Burt Walsh, and Kathy Walter

ISBN, print ed.   9781634628686
ISBN, Kindle ed.   9781634628693
ISBN, ePub ed.   9781634628709
ISBN, PDF ed.   9781634628716

Library of Congress Control Number: 2020938171

Contents at a Glance

Contents

Acknowledgments

It is not possible to put together a jointly authored published work without lots of help. We want to thank all who contributed, with a few special recognitions.

From Peter (peter@datablueprint.com)
As usual, I must thank the multitude of data professionals with whom I have worked, played, and interacted over the past decades. Each conversation has contributed to these ideas and helped to move organizations in the right direction! I remain forever indebted to my wife, Cathy. Beyond her usual editing and coaching roles, she provides the right balance of work and fun as we juggle our crazy, multifaceted existence.

From Todd (artfultodster@gmail.com)
Thanks to my federal, state, and industry colleagues who strive to make data the asset it truly is. I also want to thank my best friend and business partner, Mike Morehouse. His imagination, enthusiasm, and support are without comparison. However, I want to thank my wife, Roxanne. As I've said many times, I have never met a more remarkable woman, and I consider myself the luckiest man to share my life and ventures with her.

From Ed (eckelly512@gmail.com)

Many thanks to all the individuals who have contributed to the success and joy I have been fortunate to experience throughout my life. Special thanks to my wife, Kathy, for her never-ending love and support, and to my sons, Sean, Matthew, and Scott, for providing a father with the greatest sense of love, pride, and accomplishment. I'd also like to thank Mary Lauderdale, retired CIO for the Texas Department of Public Safety, for giving me my first state government opportunity and for being my lifelong mentor and friend.

From Burt (walshburt@gmail.com)

I would like to thank my wife, Kathy, and my kids Lincoln and Liam, for their love and making my life fulfilling.

From Kathy (kathy@nsoma.com)

I would like to thank my parents, Frank and Barbara Walter, for always supporting me.

Thanking Some Others

We also want to acknowledge and thank the reviewers listed below who generously donated their time and contributed to the critical evaluation of this book: Patrick Hannon, Adita Karkera, Kevin Lynch, Raivo Murnieks, Geoffrey Ross, and Kathy Rondon.

Last, thank you to our colleagues at Hih7 Webtech. Their artistic team produced amazing design concepts for this book. We are confident their stunning visuals will help our readers develop a deeper appreciation for data management and CDOs. We encourage readers to visit their website and learn more about how their firm could help. You can reach the Hih7 team at www.hih7.com.

About the Authors

Peter Aiken

Peter Aiken, an acknowledged Data Management (DM) authority, is an Associate Professor at Virginia Commonwealth University, past President DAMA International, and Associate Director of the MIT

 International Society of Chief Data Officers. For more than 35 years, Peter has learned from working with hundreds of data management practices in 30 countries, including some of the world's most important. Among his ten books are the first on CDOs (the case for data leadership), the first describing the monetization of data for profit/good, and the first on modern strategic data thinking. International recognition has resulted in an intensive schedule of events worldwide. Peter also hosts the longest-running DM webinar series (hosted by dataversity.net). In 1999 (before Google, before data was big, and before data science), he founded Data Blueprint, a consulting firm that has helped more than 150

organizations leverage data for profit, improvement, competitive advantage, and operational efficiencies.

Todd Harbour

Todd has over 30 years of government and business experience and is a recognized data expert and business leader. As a government executive, Todd was the Chief  Data Officer (CDO) for New York State and CDO for the Directorate of Science and Technology (DS&T) at the Central Intelligence Agency (CIA), where he led the development and operation of big data analytics capabilities across government. Todd also led many data initiatives that set up rules of engagement, decision rights, and accountabilities for the effective management of data assets. As an industry expert, Todd served as the Vice President of Federal Services for FGM for over 15 years, building the company's Federal and international practice and helping FGM achieve a successful exit in 2012. Todd is also an Associate Director of the MIT-based International Society of Chief Data Officers and a member of the Data Management Association (DAMA). Todd is the author of two books and several papers on data management and data leadership, including the first book on modern strategic data thinking. His latest book offers real-world recommendations to executive data leaders.

Todd is a certified Project and Program Management Professional (PMP and PgMP), and Chief Information Officer (CIO) with the Project Management Institute and the National Defense University, respectively. Todd is also a certified Data Management Professional (CDMP) and Data Governance and Stewardship Professional (DGSP) with the Data Management Association (DAMA). Todd currently holds four graduate degrees in information systems, project management, business administration, and government information leadership.

Ed Kelly

Ed Kelly has over 30 years of experience in business and information technology. He currently serves as the

Statewide Data Coordinator for the Department of Information Resources (DIR). In his role, he works with agencies and institutions of higher education to collaboratively develop data policies, standards, and best practices to improve data governance

and integrity statewide. Ed is also responsible for seeking out opportunities for data sharing across government agencies, to increase government transparency, reduce duplicative information collection, and improve data management and analysis.

Prior to joining DIR, he held positions with the Texas Department of Agriculture as Chief Administrative Officer and with the Texas Department of Public Safety as Chief Information Officer. Ed's experience includes a variety of roles in the private sector, including State Street Bank and Trust Company, Fidelity Investments, Dell Computer, Dell Financial Services, and Unisys Corporation.

Burt Walsh

Burt Walsh brings over 20 years of experience in the IT  industry in various technical and management roles. He has extensive knowledge of programming languages, enterprise systems, technology frameworks, data conversion, operating systems, and design methodologies.

Prior to joining AST, Burt served as Development Lead — Cloud Services with Amazon Web Services and Principal

Software Engineer with Computer Science Corporation. Some of his earlier roles include Lead Architect with the Office of Early Learning, Lead Architect/Project Manager with the Florida Department of Law Enforcement, as well as various roles with Bank of America.

Burt holds a Bachelor of Science in Mathematics from Florida State University and a Master of Science in Computer Science.

Kathy Walter

Kathy Walter has a decade of experience managing IT projects, first as a COBOL programmer in the utilities industry, then as an IT Project Manager in a variety of

website consulting firms and the financial services industry. She also worked for nearly a decade in product management and development as Technical Product Manager at Instinet Corporation, Associate Brand Manager at Gillette and Proctor & Gamble, and Senior Product Manager for Iron Mountain. Next, she branched into the education industry working as Executive Director, Product Development, for NYC Department of Education. Kathy started her own company, Nsoma, working with schools and education companies on data and technology issues.

Kathy currently works as an attorney for the State of New York focused on issues of consumer protection and data privacy. She also works with businesses and non-profits on corporate issues, including intellectual property protection and with *pro bono* clients facing credit debt, housing, immigration, and family law matters.

Kathy holds a B.S. in Applied Math from Union College, an M.B.A. from NYU's Stern School of Business, and a J.D. with a concentration in Information Law and Intellectual Property from Fordham University School of Law. Kathy also holds a graduate certificate in Teaching English to Speakers of Other Languages (TESOL) and has been an ESL educator at Northeastern University and Cambridge Learning Center, an ESL curriculum consultant with the YearUp program in Boston, and a program developer for several teaching projects in Uganda.

Preface

The idea for this book arose from discussions we had in Boston, Massachusetts, while attending the annual MIT Chief Data Officer and Information Quality (MITCDOIQ) Symposium. We noticed that much of the conference concentrated on technology. The speakers were mainly chief data officers (CDOs) sharing their technical experiences relating to data analytics. We heard all about how easy it was for private CDOs to overcome traditional problems—like sharing and integrating data—and to quickly perform data analytics.

Throughout the conference, industry representatives told one version or another of their ability to overcome organizational forces and successfully perform valuable business analytics *ad nauseum*. They described the tools they used, the technologies they applied, and the experts involved. They described the kinds of data they used, how long the analytics took to run, and how important their findings were to leadership. *Blah, blah, blah.* To those of us attending from the public sector, rather than feel inspired, we were frustrated. After years spent trying to do similar work in our own government organizations with little progress, all we saw were a bunch of people talking about how "easy" it was. It was annoying and left us with questions such as:

- How was industry able to bring its data together faster than government?
- What were they doing that was different from what we were doing?

There were many success stories of recent data analytics implementations. Still, we realized when we listened more closely that most of the success stories were describing local or small-scale success. The stories typically involved one division or department, maybe even an entire mid-sized company that successfully implemented analytics. Across many presentations, a speaker would talk about the details and then relay how the organization was going to "continue the rollout" or "continue the growth mindset" to other parts of the organization. Even when one part of a company was experiencing success, *we* knew it was not going to be an "automatic" rollout to the rest of the company.

In the public sector, our "slower approach" comes at least partially from the idea that government is big and has many moving parts. In this way, the public sector is not so different from a large private sector company—you can start a data analytics program, even implement some technical systems, but making the project into a full-scale organizational effort is not so easily done. We also noticed that MITCDOIQ sponsors, like other data conferences around the country, was made up almost entirely of tech companies. Many of the presentations featured CDOs standing with account managers or technical implementation leads from resident technology companies who also sponsored lunch following presentations. Technology was driving the conference.

In the same way, technology has been driving data policy for companies. Companies know they must do something with the data to make it more useful, and, of course, technology partners have answers for how to do it. Data is multiplying, and so are the technology opportunities. Modern technology products have allowed companies to use more of the data already stored in their systems, but technology is also leading the charge—and the strategy. So, while public sector organizations struggle to strategically position data, they are unwilling or unable to pay for the systems that private companies bought—but that does not put them as far back of the pack as the conference first had us thinking.

Rather than continue running, organizations must stop and take a breath. No matter where you are managing data and figuring out how to develop and drive solid data strategy in your organization, are any of us letting data lead the discussion?

Are you salivating over the latest technology software or development tools that will allow you to create ever better dashboards to impress your executive team? Do you dream of new ways to represent data to your stakeholders? If you answered yes, while you are trying to get that dashboard toy to work, you may be missing valuable data sitting in another system or department.

The reality is this: we must change the conversation, not just at conferences, but also in our organizations. Bright shiny objects may look pretty, but they will not allow you to drive organizational change around data. They will not help you develop solid data strategies for implementing data sharing and meaningful analytics across an entire organization. People must do that. Allowing technology to dictate strategy can work against organizations because if you measure what everyone else measures, how can you spot an opportunity? Whether we like it or not, the world is producing data at a greater rate than ever before, and therefore more data than ever to learn from or continue to ignore. Some companies and sectors have already jumped in and are taking full advantage of the wide-open spaces— low regulatory regimes, cheap storage, broad access— though even they have more room to grow.

The issue is with those left behind; governments included. And when government organizations fall behind, constituencies are left behind as well. However, we believe there are solid lessons from the public and private sectors that can enable teams to make the dramatic shifts needed in data usage to drive real strategic change—for profit, efficiency, and beyond. The needed shift is dramatic, but it is possible. It is also necessary. Now.

Foreword

It is all about the data!

The title of this foreword comes from what my good friend and colleague, Todd Harbour, taught me while we both served at New York State's Office of Information and Technology Services (OITS). For about twelve months, I had the privilege to serve as chief of staff at NYS OITS during a time of growth and transition for this new State enterprise agency. Our year working together in 2017 was eye-opening.

Following this year of service and discovery, I can say unequivocally, that I agree with Todd's assessment; ultimately, it, and IT, is *all about the data.*

I entered the tech world unconventionally, through the side door, so to speak. I have a degree in political science rather than *computer science* and a master's degree in public administration rather than in *systems administration.* For a large part of my career, I had worked with many talented civil and structural engineers on public works projects: water systems, wastewater treatment plants, public facilities, a zoo, and a new concert amphitheater on the shores of Onondaga Lake.

How much different, I thought, could it be to work in the tech sector than the planning, design, and construction of complex public works projects, right?

I knew something was amiss when I kept hearing a similar refrain from new colleagues within the agency:

This is Matt, he's not a tech guy.

Welcome Matt, he's new to the agency, but hasn't worked in tech before.

I think he's just here to look for a new job somewhere else maybe?

In November 2012, most New York State executive agencies were consolidated into the State's new Office of Information Technology Services (OITS). The goal? A four thousand person, half-billion-dollar operation designed to streamline and improve technology services to New York's public agencies and its citizens.

The IT consolidation was the result of an effort started in early 2011 by then newly elected Governor Andrew M. Cuomo, who challenged his newly formed Spending and Government Efficiency Commission, the SAGE Commission, to reduce the cost of government while also improving citizen services.

A key priority of the Governor's SAGE Commission was the advancement of the value proposition of centralizing

IT services for state agencies. IT consolidation focused on driving down costs via the adoption of enterprise platforms and the decommissioning of agency data centers.

Notably included within the SAGE Commission's consolidation framework was a sub-recommendation to set up, for the first time in New York State, an enterprise CDO position within the management structure of the new OITS. The SAGE Commission recognized that a net benefit of consolidation would be unprecedented, centralized access to the state's substantial data assets. State agencies process millions of transactions per year, including business registrations, tax payments, safety-net program applications and payments, rental help applications and payments, bridge inspection reports, emissions monitoring data, daycare center registrations, and reporting—and the list goes on and on.

The CDO would have an unprecedented responsibility to coordinate the State's new open data initiative. The CDO would also lead the State's efforts in developing and implementing enterprise-wide data standards while also focusing on opportunities to use analytics to advance and improve the delivery of services to New Yorkers. While New York has, to its credit, been a leader through its open data initiative, it is merely a peek under the covers of the data riches that New York, and states like it, hold.

An empowered CDO could work to establish data standards and governance protocols that would protect sensitive data from internal malfeasance and unwarranted release, while also providing a fast path to interagency data sharing—leading ultimately to the release of millions of data sets that could be used by university researchers, think tanks, hospitals, and others to advance good public policy.

Of course, this sounds good in writing. I think many jurisdictions, both small and large, run into similar technological, bureaucratic, and legal obstacles as those faced by New York in advancing this vision of a data utopia.

Unlike consumer-focused tech companies, such as Apple and Amazon, good customer service is poorly-defined for government organizations or, in many cases, not defined at all. For better or worse, government agency structure limits the organization's ability to use resources and provide citizens with more efficient, less bureaucratic approaches to service delivery.

In their defense, agencies are often well-intentioned in setting up protective barriers around their systems and "their" data. Locking up data, however, behind rules and protocols should not be used as a surrogate for good cybersecurity or sound data management. Bureaucratic moats hinder the streamlining of services and the leveraging of data assets to their fullest potential.

In my view, the focus was on capital investments: boxes and wires *versus* setting up long-term governance frameworks for IT infrastructure (on-premise or cloud-based), data management, and security. While the private sector is leveraging the computing power of cloud-based resources and user data to improve service delivery through analytics, deep learning, and artificial intelligence, public agencies struggle with the most basic elements of data classification. They are often reluctant to share data sets across the enterprise due to the perception of statutory or regulatory hurdles. Or it could simply be due to the lack of incentive or means to share information across disjointed platforms.

To replicate some of the success from the private sector, however, the state must have in place state-of-the-art technology with which to in-take, process, store, and transmit massive data sets. This data must be secure and inaccessible to all but those appointed (via statute and regulation) to review, analyze, and report on such data. And the data must be clean; it must be usable in various analytical frameworks in a manner that avoids countless hours of reformatting and cleaning to run simple queries.

This is difficult in an environment where each agency, either through formal or *ad hoc* processes, designs data management strategies that do not align across the enterprise. This is, in fact, a block to good data governance, which block prevents the full leveraging of the enterprise's data assets. While well-intentioned legal teams lock data up, a CDO can and should be empowered to define, educate, and enforce strategies and pathways to share our government's rich data assets.

Both consumer and citizen demand will continue to grow for application-based, secure transactions while government IT departments fight for scarce resources to simply keep the lights on. As a consumer of government services, I want to renew my driver's license on my phone. In fact, I want my driver's license to be on my phone! I want to pay my taxes and have my tax records stored in a lifetime account. I want my children to create a single account to do business with the State of New York when they reach working age and know that account will travel and grow with them as they pay taxes, register their cars, start a business, or apply for a job or scholarships.

With the proper balance of governance between technology, security, and data management, this is an achievable goal. How do we know this? Because the private sector is already doing it and doing it well. It is time for government to catch up and balance the power between the feuding clans of the technology workforce.

I may not be a "tech guy," but I do know what is most important is not which server runs a program, or if a system runs on a mainframe or in the cloud, or if we use one security product or another. What is important is that we're using technology to improve service delivery and the lives of our consumers. As more and more agency-to-agency and citizen transactions occur over networks, the data riches that result can and should be used by government to improve service delivery to its citizens. Unlike oil, which is a finite resource that pollutes our planet, our data riches grow at exponential rates and, in time, should offer a path to a future that we can now only imagine.

Enjoy this book! It is both prompt and prescient in its views on sound data governance. I am confident you will see, as I did, that IT is, in fact, *all about the data*.

Matthew Millea
Former Deputy Chief State Operation
New York State

About this Book

"First master the facts and then distort them at your leisure."

—*Mark Twain, American Author*

Why we wrote this book

The chief data officer (CDO) is a new business role, which appeared on the scene about five to six years ago. Industry was quick to embrace CDOs, but government is only now experimenting with it. Because the job is still new and changes every day, there are no universal rules describing what a CDO should do. This lack of standardization concerns us. We believe many CDOs will repeat the mistakes made across our collective data careers. That concerns us even more. We think CDOs can learn much from each other, good and bad.

Complicating matters, data management and its current pedagogy is dense and sometimes hard to understand. It is often prepared for experts by experts, and we know that explaining these new concepts can be tricky. We want our material to reach executives, managers, legislators, and other leaders to help them understand data ideas, vocabulary, and processes. We created this book as a way of explaining how data management works in a remarkably uncomplicated way so readers can easily digest the information.

Finally, this book is not about revelations and discoveries. It is not a how-to book or an authoritative reference. It is, though, a collection of insights and advice we offer to CDOs and other leaders to help give them a head start and some momentum in their data efforts. We think our recommendations have broad application: on the shop floor, in the conference room, or even in legislative chambers. We think this book helps CDOs create data-centric value for their organization, and we encourage readers to use our ideas and recommendations in ways that work for them. Every organization and every CDO journey is different.

How to read this book

We encourage readers to use this book like an index. We tried to organize our material according to a simple outline, which aligns to the major phases of the data lifecycle. We recognize some of our observations and recommendations may apply to different topics in this book, and though we tried to remove duplicative information, we included some duplication where we think it makes sense or drives home a point.

Chapter 1: **Current Environment** describes data's confounding characteristics, the current disagreement about CDO reporting structures, the need for adaptive planning, balanced implementation, and the specific must-invent new execution models. These are necessary but insufficient prerequisites to organizationally better data use.

Chapter 2: **Data Maturity** introduces a CDO process improvement framework based on years of proven research. The Data Management Body of Knowledge (DMBOK) and Data Management Maturity Model (DMM) describe core concepts, techniques, and tactics for data leaders to use.

Chapter 3: **Integration** is a plea to delay technology investments. The current technology-first approach has produced organizations that struggle to tame investments and made several consultancies very wealthy. We outline a more evolutionary approach.

Chapter 4: **Strategic Planning** describes the key roles required to sustain data and practice improvements beyond the current leader. Ninety-five percent of data challenges are people and process challenges.

Chapter 5: **Execution** describes issues CDOs will face while implementing solutions in their organizations.

Chapter 6: **Formalization** describes some efforts in both federal and state governments that are noteworthy and deserving attention. This section primarily describes work happening in the public area, but the outcome of these efforts will affect both the public and private sectors.

CHAPTER 1

Put Data First

*"If we have data, let's look at data. If all we have
are opinions, let's go with mine."*

— Jim Barksdale, Former Netscape CEO

Imagine trying to read a book without any organizing structure. No table of contents, no index, and no list of figures, chapters, or familiar aids. Most would agree, these tools are good things and help people understand ideas and concepts. Without them, readers are confused, fumbling through random pages unable to contribute novel ideas to the work. What few realize is that these organizing structures—like chapters, tables, or indices— are forms of *metadata*, information that helps people understand and navigate information. It comes as no surprise publishers spend considerable resources perfecting metadata to make each book understandable (Covert, 2014). Like publishers, CDOs try to make information understandable, except that CDOs try to make all enterprise data understandable to everyone who needs it. One might think of a CDO's job as trying to make billions of books understandable at a glance.

Today, data holds tremendous value. We are only now understanding some of the things it can do for us, and we have only begun to understand what data is truly capable of describing. In the right hands, data can change entire industries (Steele, 2015). Just look at what Amazon and Netflix did with their recommendation services, and what Walmart did with its "old school" supply chain optimization. These examples highlight the remarkable capabilities based on existing data. Naturally, others want to duplicate Amazon-Netflix-Walmart successes.

While companies see limitless opportunity to use data to improve market offerings, there is a gap between the experienced and the inexperienced. Inexperienced organizations have the most work to do, but tech-savvy organizations have plenty of work to do as well. Even companies as sophisticated as Amazon, Netflix, and Walmart are still learning what they can do with data.

Although companies and governments create more data than ever, perfecting their performance is a challenge. They continuously examine areas that need improvement to increase profitability or deliver better public services. The risk of failure is significant, and there are billions of dollars at stake. However, success more than balances the risks involved when companies can navigate them. International Data Corporation (IDC) estimates that global data and analytics investments will surpass $200 billion per year by 2020. Here are some examples of investments for certain industries.

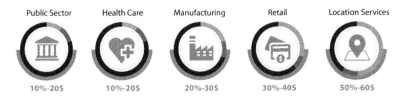

Figure 1. Types of analytics by industry sector

However, only a small percentage of organizations are taking advantage of data. Why are they having so much trouble getting value out of their data? One reason seems to be that organizations fail because they do not put data FIRST. Instead, they focus on the bright, shiny objects: technology (Carande, 2017). Technology changes captivate people. But, for technology to work, systems need syntactically correct and semantically consistent data. Even though today's technology can process unbelievable amounts of data, it is of little use without accuracy, relevance, and timeliness. Behind this work is the CDO, a role driven by organizational growth and fueled by data and data innovation (Faria, 2015).

CDOs lead, educate, motivate, and guide strategic data activities. Their plans put data first, and they shape their organization's future using data as the basis for every decision. As we shall discuss in greater detail, there is little agreement about what a CDO does. Typical responsibilities include enterprise-wide data strategy development and implementation, governance, quality improvements, and data sharing. However, if expectations surrounding data continue to rise, the danger of failure still is high.

Where are the CDOs?

Where does one find a CDO? What kinds of organizations have them? In the private sector, you can find CDOs about anywhere. They are in every country on the planet. They are in every industry. CDOs first appeared in financial organizations like banks and investment firms. Over time, other industries like healthcare, insurance, and retail have hired CDOs. Until January 2019, public sector CDOs were rare. A few forward-leaning agencies across the U.S. federal government hired CDOs. There were even fewer in local U.S. jurisdictions. Figure 2 shows U.S. public CDOs as of July 2, 2018, including states, counties, districts, and municipalities. Though there are no reliable sources, we estimate the number of worldwide private sector CDOs to be around 5,000 with only a hundred or so public sector CDOs. These estimates clearly illustrate how industry has more enthusiastically embraced CDOs and recognized the value they bring to their organizations.

Despite the difference, CDOs in both the private and public sectors share a common trait: both have disturbingly high turnovers. In fact, on average, CDOs last about 15 months in their positions (Aiken, 2017).

Figure 2. State and City CDOs

Figure 3 shows just how short some of those tenures are. Why are their appointments so short? One possible answer is that some organizational leaders see CDOs as having an *IT function* rather than a *business function*.

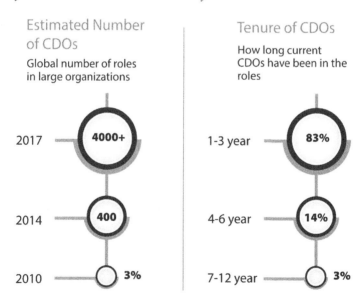

Estimated Number of CDOs
Global number of roles in large organizations

2017	4000+
2014	400
2010	3%

Tenure of CDOs
How long current CDOs have been in the roles

1-3 year	83%
4-6 year	14%
7-12 year	3%

Source: How Chief Data Officers Are Driving Business Impact, Gartner 2007

Figure 3. CDO tenure

This interpretation can have a profound impact on what a CDO can and cannot do. For example, if a CDO aligns to the business, then the CDO becomes a change agent and confronts deeply rooted organizational values and belief systems to create a new data-driven culture. However, if leadership believes data is a byproduct of IT, then CDOs typically align to the technical parts of organizations and receive a lower budget. CDOs are too often set up to fail.

Data leadership, the Red Sox, and the Yankees

Buy *versus* lease, Red Sox *versus* Yankees, public *versus* private. When it comes to managing data, there are some unique differences and challenges between public and private sectors, and those differences deserve some discussion. Many people believe that private and public CDOs are entirely different entities: one is financially driven and the other is politically or publicly driven. Often, the differences can cause dramatic strategic departures for each type of CDO. Though there may be differences, we suggest that the differences have more to do with timing and focus rather than substance.

Here is an example. In the movie, *Wizard of Oz*, Dorothy finds herself in two different worlds that are oddly connected. She was confused. She knew she was not at home, and at times felt lost, not knowing where to turn for help. In many ways, that is how the public and private sectors feel. There are clear differences, and yet, there are things that seem oddly familiar. Relying on experiences from the "other world" can lead to long-term and meaningful solutions for either sector. For instance, for several years, the private sector successfully used CDOs to its advantage. Companies recognized the value of data and how it drove their business. Commercial organizations quickly understood their success or failure was directly attributable to how effectively and efficiently they could use data.

The public sector had a dissimilar experience, however. The government did not connect data to performance the same way the private sector did. Public sector CDOs were, for the most part, figureheads and unable to affect the government's bottom line. More recently, the public sector is beginning to understand the value of data and is positioning some CDOs to succeed. Public sector CDOs are currently defining and implementing data programs that are supposed to deliver more, cheaper, and better services to the public. We expect this trend to continue as the public sector learns how to use data and improve government performance.

Additionally, at the time of writing, the private sector has begun foundational work addressing strategic data development. For example, many companies are building data capabilities to help follow new laws like the General Data Protection Regulation (GDPR) and the Health

Insurance Portability and Accountability Act (HIPAA) (Zaidi et al, 2018). Even though these companies are managing their data to support legal compliance requirements, companies can also realize collateral benefits. For example, once companies have an accounting of their data, they can better control the number of copies they use across the enterprise. No longer would each corporate division use individual copies of data. The company would, instead, be able to implement ways to use common enterprise copies of data, thereby reducing the number of copies and the cost associated with each one. If companies used enterprise data, they could exert better control over regulated information like personally identifiable information (PII), personal health information (PHI), and other sensitive data.

Some public sector organizations are working hard to get control of their data as well. For example, the State of Arkansas is a great example of a public sector organization that has begun cataloging its data assets to set up a baseline understanding of what data the state has and what data needs better control and protection. The federal government shares this concern as well. Starting in 1934, Congress set up the National Archives to preserve and care for the records of the U.S. Government. Previously, the federal government kept its records in various basements, attics, and abandoned buildings. At that time, the government had little concern for security or storage conditions. In 1935, the National Archives began to survey federal records and move documents to a new building in Washington, DC.

Today, the National Archives preserves records that have continuing value using more than 40 facilities nationwide. Also, the National Archives manages a formidable number of records: 10 billion pages of text records, 12 million maps, charts, and architectural and engineering drawings, 49 million still and aerial photographs and graphics, 300,000 reels of motion picture film and more. But, how does the National Archives keep track of it all? Let's look at a tool they have developed to help manage sensitive data.

To help improve data sharing while controlling sensitive information, NARA created the Controlled Unclassified Information (CUI) Program. 32 CFR 2002 describes all CUI rules. The program standardizes the way the federal government and its partners share data. The CUI Program sets up standards and best practices built on existing law, regulations, and agency policies to replace a legacy of inconsistencies in safeguarding and handling sensitive information. CUI standards address data across the entire data lifecycle from creation through final records disposition. The program also sets up consistent protections while easing authorized information sharing. The federal regulation also directly affects any authorized recipient of federal data, including states, counties, local government, academia, and business.

The CUI Program sets the standard all organizations must use for sharing federal data. Many groups access federal data or supply data to the federal government. A benefit of the standard is everyone understands what the data is, why it is sensitive, and how recipients can use the data. The standard is easy to understand and puts recipients on notice as to what rules apply for using each data asset. Also, the standard is extensible to other jurisdictions like states, academic institutions, and even companies. Adopting this standard makes sense for many organizations, especially those that do business with the federal government. (Learn more about NARA at https://www.archives.gov)

As the Beatles say: Come Together

Organizations come in a variety of shapes and sizes, but often, in the case of government, the structure has been set in stone or statute with siloed purposes based on a statutory and regulatory foundation for a given department or agency. For example, issues related to health belong to the Department of Health, issues related to transportation belong to the Department of Transportation, and issues related to education live with the Department of Education. Seems pretty simple, right?

So, what happens when you have an issue related to education for certification of transportation engineers who work for hospitals? Yeah, good luck with that. Ideally, government agencies would share information about these people, their certifications, hospital facilities, and more.

In the private sector, if a company's business supplied certification training for transportation engineers working at hospitals and other healthcare facilities, the organization would focus on making that exchange as efficient as possible to increase profitability. Companies can easily centralize and decentralize parts of their organization to achieve maximum results as they believe proper. For instance, a company could have a separate marketing team solely focused on education certification, but the sales force could sell education certification and online education for other employee training programs. Later, if the certification business is hopping, the company could further divide the sales force so that there are separate organizations focused on each of the two lines of business, certification training, and online employee education. If the market is not doing well, the company has other options available to it. For example, the company could train its sales teams to sell three or more types of products.

When the business needs to change, companies can quickly move and create new opportunities that cross seemingly different business areas. Additionally, companies can often make all their decisions. Sometimes companies must consult or coordinate with government officials but not all the time. Companies can make unilateral decisions about staffing, offerings, and more.

This is not the case with government. If the public sector wants to make changes, there is often a huge amount of political swirl. What services will the government provide? Who will receive the benefits of those services, and who will pay for them? These are complicated questions, and equities drive the debate. The decision-making is public and takes considerable time. If issues arise in the public sector, CDOs must learn how to navigate complex political waters. In some cases, public-sector CDOs must secure support from legislators and help shape public law. And we all know how quickly that happens, right?

The data management solution

What these scenarios suggest is a unified enterprise data management capability, including more than a stack of technologies or a few isolated analysts crammed into cubicles staring at screens. Focusing on technology to the detriment of data and the business is a losing proposition.

Take a different view: data is the lifeblood of the organization, incorporated into all key decisions across all core business functions, and led by the CDO.

The CDO helps the business use its data as a strategic asset to drive value and increase profitability. The CDO establishes and leads activities to ensure that data is ready to use. Policies, programs, strategies, and organizational structures defined and guided by the CDO help the business perfect efforts and innovation. The CDO guides and the chief executive officer (CEO) sponsors these efforts across organizational verticals. Business profit and growth rates are vital indicators of the effectiveness of the CDO's efforts (Desjardins, 2018). While CDO functionaries have grown into a more centralized organizational role recently, many executive levels still consider the position to be a technical job.

However, this is not where the CDO role began. Day-to-day operations involved data processing managers working to improve the quality and application of data. As some organizations realized they were spending a lot of money on technology, they also recognized there might be valuable data within those systems, data the organization could mine for business purposes and sensitive data that requires protection. Much of the newer data lived in systems, so data management naturally shifted under the umbrella of IT. And since IT already has responsibility for technology risk management, IT took over data management as well. Guess what came next? You guessed it—more technology solutions: dashboards and analytics.

Understand your roots

Data management is a new and immature discipline. We trace the data profession back to Ada Lovelace, the world's first programmer. Nearly 200 years ago, Lovelace realized the simple weaving loom could help solve mathematical equations. Lovelace's discovery is the precursor to every modern computing. Though data processing evolved at remarkable rates, data management did not advance at the same speed. In contrast, accounting is an old and mature discipline. Accounting has existed for almost 8,000 years as a recognized occupation. Today, accountants subscribe to a standard known as the Generally Accepted Accounting Principles to help organizations manage money according to universally respected rules (Bragg, 2018).

Because data management is an immature discipline, you will be defining the data practices for your organization. It is best to understand this upfront. You will be making some of this up as you go. We recommend you rely on Douglas Hubbard's guidance (Hubbard, 2010):

- Measurement is a reduction in uncertainty.
- Formalizing stuff forces clarity.
- Whatever your measurement problem is, it has been done before.
- You have more data than you think.
- You need less data than you think.
- Getting data is more economical than you think.
- You probably need different data than you think.

Don't feel you must go deeply into any of these areas, just have an appreciation for the origin of the discipline. If you think this way, you are more likely to develop a better appreciation for your current challenges. Recognize, too, data management is about change, and change can sometimes appear to be deceivingly simple: flashy charts and graphs showing all the wonderful things an organization will be able to do can light your imagination. Remember, though, at the end of the day, you must deal with people, and it takes more than sexy charts to change an organization's culture. Don't get us wrong, change management does have a place in helping organizations improve, but be wary about hiring someone else to help change the organization and adopt a data management strategy—that's your job!

Be aware, too, of vendors who will urge you to do something entirely different for problems that their technology solutions can solve. "It is easy," they will say. "Virtually no work at all. Just click here, here, and here and, voilà, done!" Remember: new CDOs rarely have the staff, budget, or organizational trust to sustain these sorts of tools and their implementations. So, stay focused on the basics. Understand the problems your organization is trying to solve and define how that will happen. Then, and only then, find the technology to help. There will always be a new solution or system out there, but you must use technology to enhance your work once you have defined it, not the other way around.

Another suggestion: be wary of those promoting cookie-cutter "recipes" and easy solutions to complex data management problems. Easy answers typically lead to data and governance problems or limitations that later lead to increased costs and confusion. Simply put, data management is not an assembly task where you connect two things to make everything work. If the answers were that easy, we would have a lot more CDOs!

There are usually many ways to solve a problem, but some are more difficult to implement than others. Navigating the landscape, selecting the right tool, and implementing it is what a CDO does every day. As it turns out, organizations practice data management in many ways, with no universal solution prescription. Carving out new paths and directions require starting with detailed knowledge, skills, and abilities, and flows from there. The good news is that not all solutions must come from you. Be alert! You never know where answers will be hiding!

Understanding where your power lies, who owns the decisions, and how receptive people are to your message is critical to defining a winning and sustainable strategy. It can often take as much time to find strategies to handle all the stakeholders, authorities, and external influences as it can to execute and implement your project. However, large programs need executive buy-in and executive board approval (the legislative body of the organization).

Often products and changes may require more support from a governing board. And many products and services have legal and regulatory schemes with which they must comply. The point? Understand your environment, no matter the sector. Once you know the operating environment, develop a plan for navigating them all.

Various sources of authority and direction present challenges to CDOs. People will point to different authorities to justify their behavior. Also, if there are different authorities involved, confusion can quickly follow if they want to drive separate directions. These competing authorities sometimes delay work. When this happens, people get an "out" and permission to not comply or complete work.

Last, when you do have successes, make sure you reference the work prominently in future budget requests and requests for refinement of authority. Success stories will help confirm your promulgated long-term strategy. If it helps, find ways to reflect them in the executive dashboard, thus making sure people see them!

Keep your eye on the ball

Like many leaders, both public and private CDOs divide attention across many issues. For example, one day a CDO must contend with data collection issues, and the next day, the CDO must resolve a data preservation problem. On another day, a CDO must scrutinize legal language in a data-sharing agreement as well as analyze data formats and structures. Welcome to the C-suite.

Both private and public CDOs are bombarded with a wide array of issues every day. And staying focused through these issues can be tricky, even daunting at times. CDOs must balance the work while always expecting change. Data is part of everything modern organizations do, and because data is integral to operational and strategic activities, CDOs must quickly develop methods to manage the chaos. For example, because CDOs need experts to lead different initiatives, knowing what people know is crucial information to CDOs. Both private and public CDOs also must set work priorities. Because not all work is equal, CDOs must identify high-priority work as soon as possible.

Stick to your knitting

Stakeholders ensure that both public and private sectors are held accountable for performance. But those stakeholders use different methods and standards to assure accountability. In the private sector, stockholders ensure that companies meet financial goals. Boards of directors give guidance to the corporation and adjust direction when necessary. In the public sector, however, accountability is not as straightforward. The public sector typically relies on a set of systematic checks and balances to ensure the government evenly distributes power. This approach divides power among elites with competing interests and enables one group of elites to check the power of others.

Therefore, private CDOs should understand how data affects a company's financial performance. Private CDOs should also prepare data-focused value propositions for corporate officials to convey how data and its management affects corporate performance. Public CDOs should also prepare materials describing how data affects government operations. CDOs from both sectors should be prepared to support oversight from boards of directors and legislative bodies.

Cost of doing data business

In the post-big data era, we can fully understand that technology makes up only 5% of challenges to organizational data efforts. The other 95% of the challenges are people and process-oriented and not technology problems. This may seem overwhelming, but there is good news: the disciplines of change management and organizational behavior have years of best practices available for application to your data efforts.

Therefore, organizations must manage data assets as a program to be efficient and effective. CDOs should understand data and IT are notably different from each other, and for data programs to succeed, CDOs must ensure that data efforts are separate from, external to, and precede system development life-cycle activities. For example, human resource (HR) functions are not projects. They do not have a beginning, middle, and end. No one asks when the HR will finish helping employees. HR is a function that ends only when the organization goes away. However, this sentiment is not the same for data—at least not right now.

Organizations must view data programs the way they view HR, a dedicated organizational resource dedicated to solving data problems. Transforming existing haphazard data practices into something as recognizable as HR should be a goal for all data programs. And, like HR, your organization will no longer need its data program when your organization no longer needs data. Short of that, you need data addressed at a program level that uses professional administration to make up for past neglect.

How sausage gets made

Organizations need budgets in both the private and public sectors. Organizations must know what money is available and develop a plan describing how they plan to spend that money. Sounds simple, right? Anyone who has ever taken part in the budgeting process might have something to say on this topic. Much contention exists when considering how organizations spend money. Simply put, people have different ideas as to how organizations should spend money. When this happens—and it happens a great deal of the time—things get hot. Trust us on this one.

The public and private sectors build their budgets in unusual ways. Ordinarily, the private sector sets its budget using revenue and projected financial growth. The public sector sets its budget using operational estimates and expected costs for new initiatives. A legislative body typically receives a proposed budget from an executive body and examines and discusses the proposal. The legislative body makes modifications and votes to finish the budget. A finalized budget in the public section is only partially based on expected revenues, such as taxes.

When both sectors have approved budgets, organizations are not yet out of the woods. They may still have money problems. Sometimes, leaders move money from one organization to another, resulting in deficits, surprising organizations, and introducing financial challenges through the spending year. Sadly, this is a regular occurrence. Therefore, CDOs must expect organizational change. They must prepare for budget cutbacks. And they must verify spending priorities so they can keep working with minimal disruption. Most importantly, however, CDOs must show how managing data directly contributes to improving the financial health of their organizations.

You've got a deal

Every organization needs to buy material goods and services. This is true for both private and public sectors. And both sectors use contracts as the mechanism to buy those things. Despite their similarities, however, there are noteworthy differences between the sectors.

When it comes to contracting, the private sector moves fast. And because profit drives the private sector, time is money. Consequently, the private sector can streamline procurement methods that make procurement cheaper. While cutting redundant and expensive steps makes the overall system more efficient, such optimization translates into less time and fewer dollars for each acquisition. In the public sector, things are different. Governments ensure that companies have an equal opportunity to compete for government contracts. Over the years, the public sector developed complicated rules describing how companies compete. These rules make sure everyone competes fairly while ensuring that the government gets what it needs. However, the public sector's methods typically result in higher costs and longer delivery times.

An excellent example of a public sector contracting system is the federal government's Federal Acquisition Regulation (FAR), which imposes a uniform, government-wide method for executive agency procurement contracts. The FAR strives to minimize administrative operating expenses; to conduct business with integrity, fairness, and openness; and to fulfill public policy goals. The federal government struggled for some time to control spending costs and shorten delivery times. By law, all federal agencies must follow the FAR (General Services Administration, 2013). On the other hand, the public sector has no equivalent: it is every company for itself.

Public sector CDOs must be familiar with applicable contracting requirements and develop strong relationships with contracting experts. Private sector CDOs must do the same thing but also be prepared for contracting rules to change within the company.

Key takeaways

- **Celebrate wins.** Things will get sticky and sometimes will get stuck. Celebrate wins when you see them, whether because of your team or because of others.

- **Keep moving.** Adjust as you go and keep moving! Do not spend too much time contemplating your next move.

- **Brag a little.** Show the work you are doing as you do it, so people can see where they can add value.

- **Do not be afraid to change your mind.** Be bold! When you pivot and adjust for course corrections, it shows you can admit when things are going off course and still find solutions.

- **Remember where you were.** Looking back often helps us going forward. Sometimes learning from earlier misdirection leads to a better direction in the future.

- **Use your time wisely.** CDOs can use the new-hire probationary period to weed out poor performers early.

- **Look inside.** Data-degreed individuals can command attention from multiple private company suitors, leaving public sector CDOs to grow talent from within the agency.

CHAPTER 2

That's the way we do it

"In God we trust. All others must bring data."

— W. Edwards Deming

Congratulations. You want to use your organization's data to support your mission, and you have concluded you need a data management program. Now what? Well, it's time to get serious. CDOs must understand the environment in which they work. They must understand the forces in play and how those forces affect data management. What is most important, though, is that CDOs must put data at the forefront of the business—whether that business is for profit or the public good.

To be successful, CDOs must be constant advocates for their vision and make a convincing business case for their work. This can be challenging as the environment is usually risk-averse with a conservative adherence to well-established business processes. With each step, CDOs need to gauge the organization's ability to change and be prepared to use all available tools to coax and cajole stakeholders toward thinking strategically and developing an enterprise data management solution.

Through the looking glass

There are many jokes about how the government runs. Many people in industry would be surprised at how much work it takes to get something done in government. When people change careers between private and public sectors or vice versa, they often describe the experience as "falling through the looking glass" or some other fairytale-like reference. We have experienced this phenomenon throughout our careers, and yet we believe the lessons learned are applicable in either sector. Therefore, we think it is essential to understand the similarities between the private and public sectors and give some context for those similarities. We believe this approach can lead to a better understanding of the two worlds and how CDOs can use the professional experience gained in the other sector.

We ain't so different after all

People often think that the private and public sectors differ widely. The opposite is true. At first glance, the public sector has many different sources of authority, many visions, and many stakeholders. There are laws and regulations, policies, orders, and other drivers for work throughout government. Private sector organizations have similar drivers. For example, large programs need executive buy-in and executive board approval as well.

Companies must follow internal rules and policies, as well as external laws and regulations.

Change is common in both sectors, and those proposed modifications require oversight, discussion, and approval. So, do not dismiss the other sector too quickly. Instead, look to the other side for ideas and inspiration. The other sector may call your problem something else, but chances are, they have the same issue. They might even have a solution you can use too.

Three Ps and a T

Any organization wanting to set up a long-term sustainable data management initiative needs to address four critical elements at every step in their decision-making process. These elements reflect different perspectives of decision-making that affect the organization, the CDO, and the role's success. These perspectives stand for the intersection of four powerful forces that affect virtually every aspect of CDO's world.

The forces include policy, people, process, and technology (P3T). The first P is POLICY, the rules defining how the organization controls its data and what laws are right for its legal, ethical, and moral use. PEOPLE, the second P, describes a professionalized workforce that understands the value of data and that can work across the organization by effectively using data to the benefit of the organization. The third component, PROCESS, not only provides a structure for reviewing and acting on requests for data access and improvement, but also describe how organizations orchestrate activities to use and exploit data advantages. Processes also name decision owners under certain circumstances. The last part, TECHNOLOGY, refers to the computing environments in use by organizations to collect and process data.

POLICY
Data silos are proliferating on the cloud, making it harder to find and share good data.

PEOPLE
About 60% of new business intelligence initiatives will fail to get off the ground.

PROCESS
Knowledge workers waste 50% of their time searching for data, correcting mistakes, and looking for the right people to confirm the data they do find is trustworthy.

TECHNOLOGY
Data scientists spend 60% of their time cleaning and labeling data, rather than using it to drive new insights.

Figure 4. The Four P's

The P3T construct explicitly reminds us that the most unpredictable and challenging consideration is PEOPLE. People are the glue binding all the components. It takes people to make sure that everything works in concert. Unfortunately, however, people can also easily derail any process, platform, or policy that you work to create.

A primary lesson, here, is that not every problem has a technology-based solution. We rarely see organizations that would not receive help from a balance of P3T in their solution. What organizations must do is focus data strategy on those business outcomes that help the organization exploit data across the entire digital landscape—from acquisition to final disposition, creating value in the form of innovation, customer engagement, and growth. These characteristics combine to guide the organization's data governance program. Putting it another way: your data strategy needs to be 1) actionable and support a valid and useable organizational strategy and 2) easily understood by everyone in the organization, including business and IT.

Get the organization ready for change

Is an organization ready for a CDO? To prepare an organization for change, CDOs should consider using the P3T (People, Processes, Policy, and Technology) method. If CDOs want to improve data management, they must gain control over the following. (Aiken & Harbour, 2017):

- Structural shifts in the responsibilities of some key executives

- Recognizing the challenge of interviewing competent candidates

- Fundamental changes to implementing and coordinating business and IT initiatives

- A disciplined approach to data strategy, its sequence, and its dependencies

Fortunately, the field of change management is well-researched, and there are excellent models for organizations to follow. One such model, Mary Lippitt's diagnostic tool, *Managing Complex Change* (originally published in 1987), has served us well (Lippitt, 2003).

Dig a little

Getting a data management program going is difficult, to say the least. Effective data management requires a culture that puts data at the forefront of the business, whether the business is for profit or public good. A crucial part of this work is making the organization ready for change, and setting up a "data first" approach can help get the organization ready for success. We recommend CDOs understand how well their organizations manage their data before making any changes. In our experience, very few organizations manage data at an enterprise level. Few recognize the potential of their data, and fewer have matured processes that allow them to make the best use of their data holdings.

We also found many organizations present themselves well. People do a bang-up job telling you all the great work they are doing, and they seem to be mature. Take a closer look. You will be surprised by what you see. It is common for organizations to show different levels of data maturity at the same time. We see this repeatedly. So, be ready to find contradictory information as you talk to people in your organization. Do not take their feedback at face value. Dig some. Ask questions about data management best practices and how your organization applies them. Questions like these will help you get a true understanding of where the entire organization is and how you can formulate a plan to make improvements.

Getting things going

As we have mentioned, the challenges to setting up a data-driven organization seem different for public and private sector organizations. At least at the outset. Examining each sector may show some unique issues, but the underlying frames, their intent, and related problems are not so different. What both sectors share is a difficulty getting data management efforts started in their organizations. Everyone is set in their ways, and many do not understand what data management intends to do. These are powerful counter forces for CDOs to overcome. The amount of energy necessary to get things going is significant. However, some techniques can help CDOs from either sector to get things going.

First, talk. Discussion with stakeholders, colleagues, and data management champions help CDOs establish a baseline understanding of what the organization must do with its data. Open and frank conversations supply opportunities to learn about problems, create trust, and reinforce the CDO's evolving vision. Remember, culture is not a collection of projects or the latest whiz-bang technologies. Culture is a set of social behaviors and norms that include things like knowledge, beliefs, rules, customs, capabilities, and habits.

Trust us when we say that overcoming cultural challenges is the hardest problem for CDOs and data management. And changing culture is by far the biggest barrier to getting a data program started. Despite this difficulty, CDOs can communicate all the time. CDOs can take advantage of every conversation to deliver and reinforce their message. So, take the lead from the U.S. Military: tell them what you are going to tell them. Tell them, and then tell them what you just told them.

Another powerful technique to help CDOs get things going is gaining organizational commitment. We are not talking about some simple good-faith gesture, but a real backing. For example, to make data programs hugely successful, executive leadership needs to delegate authority and funding to CDOs. Anything short of absolute endorsement will lead to almost no effect in improving an organization's data. It will be business as usual. Pay attention. This kind of commitment is hard to find, especially when organizational change is involved. There are equities and interests at stake, and when CDOs do not receive explicit decision-making power and funding, organizations often regress to parochial and baronial behaviors that block any organizational change. If this sort of behavior happens, CDOs must have the confidence of knowing they have C-suite support to break through organizational loggerheads. We discuss this problem more in Culture Eats Data for Breakfast.

Teach, learn, grow

Like other fields of study, data management requires a reliable and comprehensive educational foundation. Organizations need solid foundational data management practices if they are to effectively and efficiently use data. For example, organizational standards should guide the acquisition, processing, storing, and sharing of data assets. Without underlying core services and capabilities, organizations at every level will only continue to invent a mishmash of ways to do things—to the detriment of the enterprise. Therefore, it is incumbent upon every CDO to ensure all participants, not just the data management team, increase the organization's data literacy. A shared understanding of data management principles is essential for being able to use data across the enterprise. Ensuring data literacy is not an easy task. Because few people within leadership circles are qualified to manage data, organizations are in a delicate and precarious predicament. Until academia develops a data curriculum, organizations bear the full cost of poor data literacy.

Data literacy refers to a person who 1) recognizes data in context; 2) understands how data is created, acquired, processed, and stored; 3) tracks and accounts for data; 4) exploits data for personal and professional use; and 5) recognizes the ethical use of data, big or small. Outside of a few notable programs, there are few ways for people to learn the principles of data and data management. Our educational systems treat data as a technical discipline, and there are virtually no courses in our academic institutions teaching students how to manage a large amount of complex data. The result is a workforce that is data illiterate.

Organizations whose workforce is data illiterate present an especially difficult problem for CDOs. Improving an organization's data literacy is an ongoing effort. It never ends, and it requires attention and resources. One typical CDO goal is to help the organization become data-literate. CDOs must realize they must educate the entire workforce and not just selected parts. There are four main audiences for data literacy training:

- Executives
- Program or business leadership

- Information technology personnel
- Data practitioners

Compounding matters, organizational leadership does not realize that data management grounds enterprise architecture and systems engineering, not software development or other IT project-based work. When organizations think this way, two very costly things happen: 1) organizations treat data management as a part of individual projects, and 2) business expects IT to solve data problems. What organizations should do, however, is ensure that data management professionals work together with business and abstract their needs into actionable data requirements for the enterprise.

The following sections briefly describe issues related to key organizational roles.

Executives

Organizational executives typically sponsor an overall data literacy program. Their training focuses on how to lead with data, how to highlight and grow the program, and how to align the organizational goals with the data goals. The CDO needs to convey an understanding of the steps required not only to be successful, but to sustain the CDO's objectives. Executives are terribly busy individuals. Their time is valuable, so CDOs should supply training that makes the best use of an executive's time.

Program and business leadership

Program and business leadership is the business, its strategy, and operations. These people are typically data owners. CDOs should provide training that helps data owners understand what ownership means, how they can lead with data at a program level, and how they can attract and keep the data talent needed to develop and sustain a data-focused core. CDOs can supply more training to inform leaders of the overall data method, including the steps, stages, and support of the business goals. Of note, we encourage CDOs to include data ethics training, which focuses on practices and privacy.

Information technology leadership

Information technology leadership handle setting up and supporting IT infrastructure. They need data literacy training too. Because data programs are still unclear in many organizations, IT continues to work as they always have. No one has told them otherwise. CDOs should use data literacy training to help change culture and behaviors in this area and create new lines of responsibility across the organization. CDOs will meet resistance, however. Business experts may not step up the challenge, and IT may not step down. For businesspeople, IT has always done this work. For IT people, this is part of their job, and someone is trying to take it away.

Businesspeople must understand they are the decision-makers, and IT people must understand they are a support service. You can be sure this will not be a popular position for CDOs. We recommend CDOs deliver courses that describe why business decisions belong to the business. Like the other groups, CDOs should deliver tailored training to IT experts, including paying special attention to data management, data ethics, and privacy.

Data practitioners

Data practitioners are data analysts, architects, and scientists who work with the data on a day-to-day basis. This group is composed of experts from both the business and IT sides, and practitioners generally have strong technical skills. Their goal is to help the organization understand their data, name trends and anomalies, and visualize data for understandable consumption.

Technical experts often learn the latest programming languages and experiment with the hottest technologies. Together, these capabilities help practitioners mine data for critical insights to help executives make informed business decisions. Because these experts hold positions of trust, we suggest CDOs spend extra attention here on delivering data ethics and privacy training.

Key takeaways

- **Take the first step**. Realize your data is valuable to your organization. Understand data is a universal problem.

- **Bridge your organization**. Use data across the entire organizational landscape including policy, people, process, and technology.

- **Talk. Talk. Talk**. Meet people and understand their data problems.

- **Improve data literacy**. Assess the data literacy of your organization.

CHAPTER 3

Growing up Data

"Without continual growth and progress, such words as improvement, achievement, and success have no meaning."

—Benjamin Franklin

Outside of several notable programs, there are few ways for people to learn the principles of data and data management. In most cases, educational systems treat data as a technical discipline. Students learn to program on the first day of class but do not learn data analysis or data strategy. Today, STEM (science, technology, engineering, math) programs do not teach scientific, research, architectural, or engineering principles that constitute data management, and few students graduate with a firm understanding of data theory.

When academia does not supply the foundational knowledge, skills, and abilities to students, organizations have few options. They need data management professionals who understand data and know-how to manage it for business purposes. So, with almost no qualified applicants, organizations do what they must with the choices they have. Most often, organizations name an IT expert to the chief data position. When data practitioners are not proficient in data management, they learn about data strategy on the job and refine data theories based on firsthand project experience. The lack of foundational data education contributes directly to IT inefficiencies—some estimates range from 20% to 40% of total IT costs (Zachman 2006).

The lack of qualified CDOs creates two notable consequences. First, too few people are data literate. In today's world of ever-increasing data, it is surprising to learn most people do not know much about data. How is it created? How is it used? More importantly, people are unaware how data affects them on a real and personal level. Second, to have a substantive conversation with data illiterate people, data management experts must translate for the other participants. Data literate people must explain data concepts and give relevant context to make sure everyone understands each other's ideas. Few people can do this well.

Today, most schools treat data management as a collection of technical industry standards and courses sprinkled across various academic programs. Schools simply ignore data management as a discipline, which is crucial for running today's data-driven organizations. And, as we have seen, educational systems turn out students who are functionally data illiterate on a wholesale basis. While this phrase may seem overly critical to some, we believe that it accurately depicts the problem.

The *Cambridge English Dictionary* defines *literate* as:

---

1. *Able to read and write*
Example: The man was barely literate and took a long time to write his name.

2. *Having a good education or showing it in your writing*
Example: He wrote a literate, colorful column, and reviewed plays.

3. *Having a basic skill or knowledge of a subject*
Example: They wanted to make sure their child was computer literate.

We can apply these definitions to data management. For example, data practitioners are literate if they understand and apply data theory. At first glance, this definition seems reasonable, but we think it too simple. Therefore, instead of describing people as being data literate or illiterate, we offer another way to distinguish someone's data literacy or proficiency level. Consider the following: many people cannot discriminate real news from a Facebook post. To distinguish real reporting from fake, consumers must be able to prove data proficiency in several areas:

- Recognizing context
- Understanding data creation
- Comprehending the value of tracking and accounting for data
- Experience exploiting data for personal and professional use
- Actively knowledge of the ethical use of data

We think that this scale accurately describes data proficiency and can contribute to a data-driven society.

Last, we see data proficiency as lacking at all levels in organizations. We see technical experts lacking in data proficiency. Some technologists work with data every day. They are intelligent people. They are experts in their fields, and they can technically manipulate data. But they are not necessarily data proficient in all data areas.

CDOs must understand how to interpret data and develop policies and plans using quantifiable evidence. They must also create opportunities for others to learn and become data proficient as well. Additionally, CDOs should share their knowledge in a non-threatening and inclusive manner, avoiding intimidating technical terms and jargon. Remember, data affects everyone's work, their products, their budgets, and more. We encourage CDOs to become fluent in data and help their organizations become data proficient.

Get smart with data—get proficient

Without uniform standards and approaches, it is impossible to expect uniformity of process or outcome. Only recently has there been a widely accepted framework for managing data. The Data Management Association's (DAMA) Data Management Body of Knowledge (DMBOK) is the leading reference for data professionals. Carnegie Mellon University's Data Management Maturity Model (DMM) is another respected framework. Together, these documents give data practitioners a huge head start for setting up data best practices in their organizations.

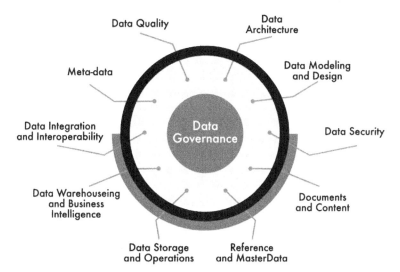

Figure 5. The DMBOK Wheel

In 2009, DAMA International published the first edition of the DMBOK. The DMBOK got its name from another popular reference called the Project Management Body of

Knowledge (PMBOK), which described project management best practices. In its second version, the DMBOK evolved into being the authoritative source for data management reference, terms, and concepts. The reference presently classifies data practices into 11 discrete data management areas.

Don't reinvent the wheel

The DMBOK is, however, best suited for small groups as opposed to individual use. To illustrate, consider the process of adding data warehousing capabilities to an organization. Warehousing falls under the DMBOK category "Data Warehousing & Business Intelligence." Yet, rarely has an organization successfully implemented these capabilities and stayed exclusively within that part of the DMBOK. Projects routinely incorporate other DMBOK disciplines like data quality and data governance.

The DMM also is the best way to document, measure, and grow your data programs. It revolves around the idea of continuous improvement and builds on decades of research and results. While all improvement efforts begin with the obligatory "assessment" phase, Carnegie Mellon's CMMI and DMM are the only proven frameworks that have the added benefit of literally decades of practice and benchmarking data (Board, 2006 and Aiken et al., 2007). Organizations not using the DMM risk comparing results against other organizations and adopting unproven methods. Thankfully, using the DMM is straightforward. Determine the current level of practice in each area on a scale of 1 to 5, decide what must happen at the next level higher, and then implement changes required to achieve higher performance.

STRATEGY	GOVERNANCE	OPERATIONS	ARCHITECTURE	QUALITY
Best practices for establishing, communicating, justifying, and funding a collaborative vision for data management.	Best practices for ensuring broad participation in the practice and senior oversight of the effectiveness of data management.	Best practices for specifying data requirements and managing implemented data across the entire supply chain.	Best practices for establishing methods and standards that successfully integrates archives, and retains data assets.	Best practices for defining and implementing a collaborative approach for detecting, assessing, and cleansing data defects.

Figure 6. DMM practice areas

Guided by these two important frameworks, all data improvements are processes—processes of increasing organizational competence for a specific aspect of data. All data management improvements usually require multiple DMBOK wedges from one specific DMM level to the next.

In both corporate and public organizations, various verticals will have various levels of data maturity, all within the same organization. The public section sometimes exaggerates the differences in the public sector with various agencies having wildly different requirements for compliance, funding, and oversight. Even with these differences, though, thinking about the organization's goal for data maturity and direction should have a repeatable process mindset at the forefront to ensure that, as data change gets underway within the organization, the organization sustains it and grows it over time.

A recipe for data

Data management best practices offer a structured way to derive value from data assets. These practices help organizations effectively "clean their room" and make data ready for other business purposes. For a complete description of what each level requires, consult the Data Management Maturity Model. Let's take a closer look at each level.

DMM level 1: It works for me

Level 1 organizations define processes in an *ad hoc* manner that works primarily at the project level. Organizations typically do not share methods across business areas. Process discipline is reactive. For example, data quality processes emphasize repair over prevention. Foundational improvements may exist on an individual basis within an organization, but those organizations do not extend them throughout an organization or keep them beyond the completion of a specific project or plan.

The name gives you a good idea of what's happening. For those working at Level 1, the world revolves around the project—individualized projects. At this level, everyone focuses on helping the plan succeed with little to no attention to the enterprise level. For many, the elements are present, but it limits them to carrying out only what is part of the project. For example, decision-making and planning vary; communications vary from project to project and from business unit to business unit. Naming conventions and standards do not exist, or ones that do exist for a project do not extend beyond their immediate use on a project. Organizations must present clear business cases for funding decisions on an individual basis.

DMM level 2: Make the same mistake at least two times in a row

Level 2 organizations have set up data policy and supporting processes. These organizations typically have dedicated data stewards that work with stakeholders to ensure that the organization follows its procedures using a systematic method. Data management exists in such organizations, but processes vary between diverse groups. In such organizations, a review of best practices measured from outcomes in separate groups can lead the organization to adopt process standardization across groups, yielding outcome predictability and helping to reduce risk when processes conflict. Following a structured and objective process across groups also helps to engender management trust and support for new initiatives, since outcomes will be a bit more predictable.

Level 2 organizations recognize that continued operation and focus at the project level is costly and counterproductive to enterprise goals. This translates into individual projects beginning to look beyond project borders and programmatically interacting with other projects. Plans start to assemble the necessary components of a strategy within business units or cross-cutting programs. Projects develop engagement models and define consistent business practices, roles, and responsibilities. Projects also set up management and become adaptable to changing business needs.

A key concept for organizations working at Level 2 to adopt is that they can make the same mistake at least two times in a row. Though this sounds silly, it is critically essential for process evolution. Consider this: If a program can make the same mistake two times in a row, it can begin to adjust and measure progress against a baseline. Eventually, the organization can repeatedly cycle to a state where it can perfect its business processes.

Once public and private sector CDOs have data programs set up and fortified with data strategies, inventories, and governance, their survival and ability to influence the organization going forward should be guaranteed. Why? The only constant is change. Even when you trigger a massive operational shift, momentum must keep it going. Internal and external threats, organizational upheaval, the dreaded internal double threat (employees and budgets)—

almost anything can derail new data management programs because such programs require extensive resources at the beginning. Building contingencies is a start but shoring up all plan aspects is critical to making progress.

As a program grows and you begin to develop policies, processes, and standards, make sure you regularly review and align the documentation. It may seem obvious to you what a program is trying to do, but it is also essential to embed that understanding everywhere. For instance, make sure policies describe what you want to do. Procedures describe how you intend to perform work, and standards describe rules by which the organization will conduct its technical work.

DMM level 3: Getting the organization in shape

Level 3 organizations have learned through practical application how best to perform different activities compared to data management. These organizations hone their processes and document them in materials that are available to the organization. More importantly, they set up codified bodies of work and methods and expect everyone to follow the standards to become more effective and efficient. When organizations follow these specific and public processes, they begin to foster organizational trust because they know what others are doing and who is involved.

Organizations continuously change, not just in strategic ways—developing a data-driven mindset and programs, for instance—but also in leadership. We can all attest to precisely knowing what we were supposed to do one day and having the world shift under us when new guidance comes to the organization. However, changes in organizational leadership can best be managed with measurements that make sense. Having key performance indicators (KPI) for every aspect of the data program can help in ensuring your data strategy ties firmly into the broader organizational goals, but also how it is embedded in several programs across the organization.

As mentioned, beware of the person who says, "measure everything." Instead, figure out what is important and measure that. Start by measuring a few aspects of the overall data program. Make sure that the metrics are correct and meaningful. Once the organization is comfortable with what the numbers show, step back and ask yourself, "What else should we measure? Where does the organization 'hurt,' what needs repair, and what can we do to fix it?"

Additionally, as you start to see successes with data delivery on a small basis, resist the urge to build solutions using these numbers. The more data people see, the more data they will want to see—but it will not be their "final answer." Once you create systems, it becomes difficult to change them. Instead, though it seems counterintuitive, use paper. Paper allows you to visualize numbers and data, or even mockup reports, using current numbers *before* trying to formulate a long-term solution or process. Take the time to "measure twice and cut once" or, in the case of data strategy, "iterate, iterate, iterate, and then iterate again." Use the time to continue collecting feedback and gather information about the essential data to make sure KPIs and resulting attempts to measure them answer the organization's questions before engaging automation.

DMM level 4: Count the things that matter

Level 4 organizations use process metrics to manage their data in terms of metrics to measure variance, predict outcomes, and analyze quantitative statistics. Level 4 organizations manage work across the entire data lifecycle.

Money may be the root of all evil, but no one complains when they get more of it. This saying applies to staffing organizations; rarely does anyone complain when organizations hire more people to help complete needed work. However, just like "mo' money, mo' problems," both employees and money can cause headaches in other, not always prominent ways. The key to shoring up your organization when you get more employees and more budget is to provide both with a smooth place to land. People are more comfortable working when they know how others measure their work. The organization feels better about how you are spending money when you estimate what you are spending it on. The two go together.

So, talk to people. Discuss problems and potential solutions. Invite others to be part of the solution.

We suggest beginning by setting up a structure. The goals you want to achieve must be measurable. Otherwise, no matter the accomplishment they stand for, no one will be able to see what you have done. Metrics help solidify where you have been, where you are going, and how close you are to getting there. Metrics also help you see when the organization stalls, loses direction, or changes course.

Once you have the metrics to measure where you are on the data organization's strategic map, you can start to see where tasks are repeating themselves. You can find processes you want to reuse, procedures that might need improvement, and processes that should go away. Where you find mutual benefit, positive directions, and conventional approaches, the more likely you are to successfully adapt the entire organization to generate such positive outcomes. More important, the organization will be less likely to adopt unhealthy habits. Formalizing standards of operations and processes can help the organization in staying on the right track. Rules give the organization direction and guidance to help when people make decisions outside the data program's control. If this happens, the organization will realize the data strategy— even in the most remote areas of the organization or for the least prioritized data elements.

DMM level 5: Data leads the way

Level 5 organizations advance by applying Level 4 analysis for target identification of improvement opportunities. Level 5 organizations are also innovative in process improvements and have a strong alignment between the use of data and business strategy. Such organizations also allow data to lead planning, which can result in the pursuit of new business opportunities. Improvement in important indicators underpinned by data and data management, yields capital to convince leadership to implement data-driven strategy and operations.

At this level, organizations are fluent in data management practices. Organizations use the right tools when they need them, and they use those tools to help them make decisions across their organizations. A distinguishing characteristic of level 5 organizations is data governance. For these organizations, data governance is an enterprise tool that helps ensure that they are managing data to reap its maximum potential.

Regardless of the organizational level where you work, understanding where the organization sits now is just as critical to the next steps as being further up the spectrum. Keep in mind: almost no organizations are at Level 5, and many may be further behind than you think.

If I am solving problems and 'fixing' what's broken, then I can balance the cost of analytics. How much more can I really spend to get how much more benefit? It turns out that this is the wrong way to consider the benefits of two other levels of data analytics.

Key takeaways

- **Don't reinvent the wheel**. There are excellent resources to use. Consult DAMA and the DMBoK for industry best practices.

- **Measure your maturity**. Use the DMM to understand your organization's data maturity.

CHAPTER 4

Focus, Focus, Focus

"Data are becoming the new raw material of business."

— Craig Mundie, Microsoft Advisor

There is a popular saying that says, "Go big or go home." That is one approach, but we do not recommend it for CDOs. New CDOs want to make a difference. They are often anxious and want to show immediate results for their organization. We recommend CDOs treat their work more like a relay race. If a CDO leaves, there will be another. Remember, data management is not a project! It is a long race with many legs. Each CDO will experience success and failure and must execute a clean handoff to the next CDO.

Some tips for success

Change takes work. There is no way around it. As people work together, they can change organizational behavior, processes, and efficiencies. Organizations can publicly celebrate their success and recognize key contributors.

New CDOs should focus on showing mass and momentum. If they do that, others will see the positive impact of their work and will support more change. One of the best ways to gain organizational momentum is by targeting short-term wins.

Target short-term wins

For those involved in organization-wide change, they know how hard it is to implement lasting change. As many have noted, change often begins with good intentions and ideas, but effort alone might produce little or no sustained change. Failure leads to finger-pointing and blame if resources disappear. Leaders find themselves with one lingering question: what just happened? So, leadership looks back. They want to know where things went wrong. The leaders did the right things. They created a sense of urgency. The organization communicated the shared vision. Leaders ensured that stakeholders were involved along the way. Despite this, however, things stay unclear. Leadership still does not know why the origination failed.

One of the most common reasons why organizations fail is because a CDO "swings for the fence." The CDO takes on too much work, makes too many promises, and does not have a comprehensive plan. The combination of these failures is a recipe for disaster. Their work bloats, and the demand for more resources grows beyond what the organization considers tolerable. And with no evidence of success, stakeholders quickly conclude the CDO has sold them a pig in a poke.

What is a short-term win? The idea is simple enough, but what does it mean? A short-term win is an organizational improvement a person can complete in six to 18 months. A short-term win is not a trick or a stunt. A short-term win is a significant but limited unit of work that has considerable value to the organization. According to Kotter, a short-term win must meet three criteria:

- Be unambiguous
- Be visible across the organization
- Be clearly related to the change effort

Short-term wins are crucial to starting and sustaining organizational momentum and help CDOs ensure stakeholders still are engaged. As we said, change takes time and significant effort; therefore, organizations must deliver short-term wins to ensure the organization continues to support the work. For example, if organizations stay focused on short-term wins, CDOs can celebrate small but essential victories and help derail cynics who prefer to keep the status quo. Small wins give CDOs something tangible they can cite to fuel excitement and cultivate a willingness to change the organization. Additionally, stakeholders can take part by finding other efforts that could be short-term wins for the organization.

Fight overcommitment

CDOs want to be successful. If something works, CDOs want recognition for their contributions. However, CDOs must be careful not to overcommitment. They must show restraint and show they can manage data in overly complex bureaucratic environments. They must fight the urge to make too many promises and spit-ball ideas. Instead, we recommend CDOs develop two kinds of plans: short-term and long-term plans. Use a short-term plan to get some early wins under your belt. Short-term wins give CDOs early credibility, which builds stakeholder trust. Remember, many stakeholders are looking at you with a cautious eye. CDOs are typically new to organizations, and people are not sure what the CDO is going to do. So, show stakeholders early success and earn their trust. For example, CDOs could find a narrowly scoped project that saves money. They could define the project to ensure a high probability of success and implement controls to fight scope creep throughout the work.

Once CDOs finished their first project, they should step back, evaluate their position, and find another short-term win. The pressure will go down over a short amount of time, and CDOs will begin to develop organizational credibility. We cannot underscore this point. You are the CDO, and you are something foreign to your organization. You must deliver early wins to secure stakeholder trust.

When CDOs succeed with one project, wash, rinse, and repeat with another. Above all: Do not overcommit!

Rack up small wins for big wins

According to author Scott Anthony, organizational transformation is a watchword that means different things depending on the context and intent (Anthony, 2016). CDOs must be able to distinguish the difference so they can pivot and turn short-term wins into larger organizational change. For some CDOs, change means doing things better, cheaper, or faster as it relates to how their organization currently works. For other CDOs, change means delivering existing goods and services in entirely separate ways. And for others, change means developing entirely new products and services. As we have said, CDOs must build momentum before they can achieve long-term organizational change, and momentum comes from focusing on short-term wins and being able to turn small wins into a mature data program.

A metaphor for organizational change is sailing. Wind is the energy that propels sailboats to a desired destination. Normally winds are predictable, but sometimes they are not. Global forces affect wind direction and intensity at times, making predictions not possible. Like real winds, global forces affect business. Most often, people can measure and predict markets, but occasionally global forces make prediction impossible. Sailors and businesspeople must respond to forces outside their control if they want to gain momentum.

Like sailors, CDOs must occasionally adjust to achieve a desired goal. For example, when winds change, sailors set their jibes to new positions. A new sail setting causes the sailboat to change course for a time. When winds change or the sailboat reaches a desired waypoint, the sailor resets the jibes to another setting, which puts the boat on another course. Changing sail settings causes the sailboat to go back and forth but allows the sailboat to hold a general course towards the desired destination. This technique is called *tacking* in nautical terminology.

Like sailors, CDOs cannot always plot a direct course. They too, must set and reset work in response to outside forces. CDOs may begin work that takes the organization in one direction and then seemingly in another direction. However, both efforts take the organization in the desired strategic direction. Setting and resetting their work keeps the data program on a steady course towards strategic goals. However, CDOs cannot just start and stop work. They must deliver wins along the way to keep stakeholders on board.

A chilly example

Out of nowhere, a massive snowstorm hits upstate New York in May. Even worse, a massive snowstorm hits after several weeks of 80-degree temperatures, and everyone has already put their snow shovels away. Contrary to widespread belief, the last snowstorms in upstate New York usually occur in April. A late-season storm like this one is a public emergency and an ideal time to have an open flow of data between the many coordinating agencies and municipalities involved in the crisis. Concerns about security in schools, places of worship, and various public venues might come into play if people are stuck somewhere.

How can CDOs position their data and make it ready to share with their traditional partners? And things also change. Maybe school districts were not in the original agreement. Now, water districts have some exciting information that, ideally, would be available to those who understand what the increase in snow might do for flooding in the general vicinity.

There are public safety concerns, but there are also organizations that need information quickly. So, CDOs should look at areas where they can rapidly share data without having to negotiate countless agreements, which would take so much time to execute that the snow would already have melted. Remember, CDOs should set up these data-sharing relationships before emergencies happen, not after.

Sell snow to Eskimos

Have you ever seen someone and thought, "That person could sell ice to Eskimos" or, "That guy could charm a snake"? Some people appear naturally gifted at getting what they want from other people. It seems like they were born for it. We think of these people as natural salespeople. As odd as it may seem, there are concrete lessons for CDOs from the world of sales.

Be empathic not sympathetic

It may surprise you to learn that sales is not all about being good at *selling*. The list of characteristics for ensuring success as a salesperson is surprisingly short. Researchers have showed two key characteristics: empathy and desire for the sale (ego drive) (Mayer & Greenberg, 2018). It turns out that when people understand another person's position (empathy, not sympathy), they find ways to convince them to do things for them (ego drive). If this happens, the ratio of success for sales tops the charts.

The first takeaway: there is a finite set of things to consider when trying to "sell" someone anything. The second take away: the first thing you should do is listen and understand what the other person needs.

Like salespeople, CDOs must learn to negotiate using ego and empathy to get what they need. For example, new CDOs must convince organizational executives to give them authority and financial resources. This is not an easy thing to do. Everyone competes for those same things. The key to getting what you want is not talking about what you want and need. Instead, the key is to focus on what others need and give people something they can use. For example, people have data, and they have operational expectations for what they should do. CDOs must understand these kinds of organizational relationships. Do CDOs know what those expectations are? Do they know ways they can discover them? Do they have something to offer the stakeholder? CDOs must be able to understand those sitting on the other side of the table and then figure out how to help them succeed.

Five P's in a pod

Here is a way to think about sales and how it relates to understanding your stakeholders: In sales, there is the concept of the four Ps. The first P is people. Who are the people to whom you are selling? What are their problems and what are their priorities? The second P is product: an understanding of what it is you are trying to sell. The third P is placement: where you should sell your product to allow people to find and buy it easily. The fourth P is position: how you should talk about your product to make it appeal to the maximum number of buyers.

Keep in contact

Marketing researcher Jeffrey Lant writes that it takes seven contacts inside 18 months to make a sale. Some argue it takes even more (1993). The exact number may vary by person, but the key point is CDOs must spend time interacting with their stakeholders so they can learn about their needs and issues. However, getting more than one meeting with a busy person may not be possible. Time is a premium for people. Therefore, CDOs must get creative. They must find ways to insert themselves into a busy stakeholders' work. The more CDOs know about their stakeholders and their data problem, the better they can find opportunities to connect with them (outside of normal meetings) and successfully offer solutions to their problems.

Practice Your pitch

Researchers have investigated communications and written how important it is to business. It bears emphasis here, particularly as it relates to CDOs. As we have discussed, organizations dedicate huge resources to organizational transformation, but success is often unsuccessful. A key contributor to failure is a lack of or simply poor communications. CDOs must understand how critically important communication is across all data efforts. CDOs must show their stakeholders they understand their problems. But more importantly, CDOs must talk the talk and walk the walk to keep that trust.

You can never communicate too much. Treat every communication effort as though it is your most significant attempt at getting the message out. People may not hear it the first time around and, when they finally do listen, they are likely to consider it to be the first time you have said anything about it. This is especially true when a leader introduces a new vision. People need time and opportunities to hear it and to separate the message from the noise of change. It takes more than one memo or speech to capture attention and build support. Intersperse the vision throughout regular conversations. Be dynamic and be intentional about continuously communicating. We believe that there are several types of messages that CDOs should develop, practice, and perfect. Depending on the audience, CDOs should change some content to ensure that the message is understandable and meaningful to the audience.

Spin a yarn for 'em

Storytelling is one of the most powerful ways for CDOs to influence, teach, and inspire people. CDOs can use stories to create connections among people and between people and ideas. Good stories make complex ideas understandable and memorable and can engage listeners in ways that PowerPoint could never do. Accordingly, CDOs can use stories to build familiarity and trust and help listeners to be more open to data management concepts (Boris, 2017).

There is solid research behind this approach. Organizational psychologist Peg Neuhauser has written that people remember information in stories more accurately and for much longer than information presented as cold facts and figures (2017). Likewise, psychologist Jerome Bruner's suggested people are 20 times more likely to remember facts if presented in story form.

In business, stories help people make sense of work, problems, and controversies. Stories connect people and are essential to setting up organizational culture. According to researchers David Kidd and Emanuele Castano (2013), stories help people understand others' mental states and enable social relationships. Moreover, stories entertain, provoke, and incite people. Sometimes, stories surprise us. They make us pay attention and look for meaning. Stories make us think and make us feel, which, in turn, helps us remember ideas and concepts in ways that numbers and text cannot do. However, there is more. According to Boris and Peterson, stories can serve many purposes:

- Establish a leadership presence
- Build a culture
- Capture and share knowledge
- Manage change
- Develop staff
- Build teams
- Sell an idea

Daniel Taylor (1997) said it best in *The Healing Power of Stories*:

> A story does what facts and statistics never can: it inspires and motivates. Expert storytellers translate complex ideas into practical examples laced with strong emotional connections. The audience tunes in because they see themselves woven into the story.

For CDOs, storytelling is a powerful tool to influence, teach, convince, and inspire those around them. For example, CDOs communicate with staff, stakeholders, and customers. CDOs interact with stakeholders in various places. Some interactions are casual, and others are formal. A formal interaction is trying to explain the different data management practices. Because data management introduces new vocabulary and presents data in new ways, many of these concepts are new and difficult to understand for beginners. A typical outcome: CDOs can have problems explaining what they are trying to do. We strongly encourage CDOs to practice telling stories about themselves and their experiences. We've seen firsthand how stories can forge new relationships, explain complex ideas, and ease controversy.

If CDOs use traditional methods of sharing information with people, they are likely to have little success. We suggest CDOs try storytelling as an alternative way of sharing information. If they do not change, people could become frustrated and just stop listening.

Words matter

At the heart of data management is something called metadata: data that gives context to another data element. For example, I ask, "What does the number 42 mean?" Without metadata, you would be clueless and have no idea unless, of course, you happened to read Douglas Adams' classic work, *The Hitchhikers Guide to the Galaxy*. Since its publishing, geeks around the world have wasted years trying to uncover some profound, symbolic significance to the number and its occurrences. When asked, however, Douglas explains that the number 42 means everything and nothing at the same time. It was a joke. The point is, though, that "42" needs context to have meaning, and, just like 42, all data needs context so that we can assign meaning and understand the values communicated.

Data sharing requires background, too. We need more context about data assets. We must name other aspects of the environments in which we intend to process, store, and use data. We also must know more facts about the people expected to use data. So, let's take a few moments and discuss these foundational data sharing building blocks.

Just like chocolate cake

Data is like chocolate cake. Perhaps that is an odd thing to say, but it is true. No one wants to share their dessert. People want to keep their favorite things for themselves. Data is not much different. Organizations (and people) love their data. They watch it, take care of it, and use it like it was some scarce resource after a global holocaust. So, sharing chocolate cake means that more people have smaller slices to enjoy. Unlike chocolate cake, however, chocolate cake is not a finite resource, and society has much to gain through sharing. What follows is a review of some common obstacles to data sharing—and some ways to overcome those obstacles.

Lines on the road

Sometimes we forget that words matter. Subtle differences exist in intent and actions that sometimes require a level of precision not currently available in our vernacular. Data management is one of those areas. When we describe diverse kinds of data sharing, there are underlying relationships that we often overlook or ignore. However, *these relationships are the very things that impede our ability to effectively and efficiently share data.* For example, when one looks at governments and how they share data, there are only a few relationships that we need to address, and they are all predicated on the idea of jurisdictions. According to the *Oxford Dictionary*, jurisdiction is an authority that has the power to make laws, rules, or legal decisions for a designated territory or group. Take a closer look at types of relationships involved and see how rulemaking plays out compared to jurisdiction.

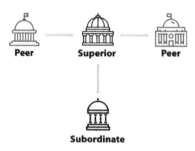

Figure 7. Jurisdictions

- **Superior:** exercises power to impose its rules over another jurisdiction. An excellent example of this is the power of the US federal government to impose controls over states without impinging on their rights.

- **Peer:** having the power to impose its rules over another jurisdiction. Connections are typically set up through treaty, agreement, contract, or some other legally enforceable instrument. For instance, several states may enter a pact to recognize and respect the rules of others to conduct commerce or some other mutually beneficial activity.

- **Subordinate:** bound to follow a superior's rules. This relationship is the inverse of superior.

Jurisdictions and the attendant power to make rules positively affect how organizations share data, and where those organizations are in the model, can severely limit the ability to influence forces in their favor. Likewise, there are different kinds of data sharing scenarios that require different types of experts to own individual decisions.

For instance, when two peer organizations share data, there is an expectation that each party will respect the rules that each attaches to their data. However, there is no practical way to ensure that each party does what it promises to do. Consequently, this type of sharing introduces increased risk and, with risk, more scrutiny, and desired assurances that the other party is truthful and trusted in the data-sharing relationship. For example, if the states of California and New Mexico decided that it was in their interest to share data, each state, typically, would promote one or more experts who would negotiate the terms and conditions of the data exchange. They would wrestle with all kinds of scenarios that would negatively affect their data and the interest of each party and its citizens. This can sometimes take months or even years to do, and, after the bureaucrats have finished talking and have shaken hands sealing the deal, each turn to their respective legal counsel, and the legal wrangling begins. This, too, has been known to take years to do—even after the organizational leaders have committed to the exchange! This is not an effective way to share data.

Risky business

And as it turns out, the language we use to describe data sharing and the decisions that go with it is imprecise. For example, most would agree that the relative risk of sharing data within a single jurisdiction is much less than sharing between two different jurisdictions. The likelihood of something going wrong if the Texas Department of Social Services shares data with the Texas Department of Taxation is much less than if the State of Ohio were to share similar data with the State of Illinois. The risk is less when two parties share data within a single jurisdiction because the jurisdiction can better keep control over data provisioning, processing, and use. Intra-jurisdictional data sharing removes that data power struggle.

Even though we conceptually recognize the difference and the risk involved in these kinds of data sharing scenarios, we do not use different words to describe them. Nearly every data sharing scenario uses the same word, no matter the sender and receiver. Organizations typically use the word *disseminate* to represent all the possible data sharing scenarios. Practically speaking, there is a distinct difference sharing data between two peered organizations in the same jurisdiction versus two parties in two different jurisdictions. Lumping all data sharing decisions under a single term introduces a significant risk of confusion to all parties.

New words

Today, everyone talks about data sharing. They talk about the need to exploit the nascent power of data. They talk about the legal complexities that go with each different kind of data, and they talk about the mission imperative to share data for the betterment of society. These are all worthwhile pursuits. They are problems that organizations must solve, but, while these conditions are necessary, they are insufficient for sharing data in a repeatable, auditable, reliable, and trusted manner. Therefore, we suggest CDOs adopt a new vocabulary, one that more precisely describes the types of data sharing. The following table is our suggested terms and definitions to describe each unique data sharing scenario.

Term	Definition	Risk
Distribute	The process of an authority giving permission to share data with an operational part within the same Jurisdiction.	Moderate
Disseminate	The process of an authority giving permission to share data with another Jurisdiction (e.g., superior, peer, subordinate).	High
Release	The process of an authority giving permission to share data with the Public.	Very Low
Dispose	The process of an authority giving permission to transfer data stewardship from an operational part to a preservation part within the same Jurisdiction.	Low

Key takeaways

- **Garner support.** Public and private CDOs will discover issues when securing the support of technical professionals. If these experts view data as a technical problem rather than a business problem, CDOs should expect resistance. Try developing training that illustrates how businesspeople can help make technical solutions easier.

- **Understand the context.** Make sure that stakeholders understand the problem. Ensure too that stakeholders share the same meanings of things. Do this as early as possible to avoid confusion.

- **Explore ideas.** Find candidate problems and make sure that everyone agrees on the priorities. Focus your effort on problems that have real benefits to the organization. Look for short-term wins. They always pay off.

- **Make sound choices.** Individuals learn in many ways. A common way is through focus and repetition. Look for ways to focus the organization on discrete problems and options. Use data governance to build organizational muscle memory.

- **Take action.** Get work done but manage the work. Keep the work focused and do not let the scope creep so that you can finish it on schedule.

- **Accept feedback.** You are going to fail at something, and the feedback may not be easy to accept. You tried your best, but you didn't get the results you wanted. We've all been there. Stay open and respectful and take the feedback. Use the opportunity to ask for ideas from people and, above all, learn from your experiences in day-to-day operations. Access and share an understanding of the problems and opportunities within the organization to create change in conversations. This also makes more people available and willing to discuss solutions.

- **Collaborate with business and IT.** CDOs must be resourceful and look to collaborate with both business and information technology. Look for and assemble a list of allies who can help advocate for program goals.

- **It is a marathon, not a sprint!** Working anywhere requires an understanding of the machine. Recognize that success comes in small steps and that the path is a long journey. Celebrate the small wins; evangelize and communicate the success of your program.

- **Advocate and advertise on behalf of your customers.** Stakeholder success is also your success!

- **Become an evangelist and the trusted resource!** Highlight the program whenever the opportunity arises; offer to speak to other management staff.

- **Listen to the other side:** Public and private sectors are alike at the core, so do not dismiss the other side too quickly.

- **Ask the tough questions.** People like to share all the great work they have done, but CDOs must ask tough questions to understand where their organizations really are.

- **Do not underestimate the power of conversation.** It builds trust.

- **Secure executive commitment and funding.** We cannot overstate how important this is. Be sure to get funding too. Without it, you are whistling in the wind.

- **End data illiteracy.** Remember, just because people have technical skills does not mean they understand data and data theory.

CHAPTER 5

Ready, Fire, Aim

*"The goal is to turn data into information, and
information into insight."*

—Carly Fiorina, Former Hewlett-Packard Co Executive

We say it several times in this book: change is hard. Saying
that may not make it any easier but refusing to
acknowledge it makes it even harder. To create a culture
that is ready to use data as a strategic asset, the
organization must make fundamental, but healthy
changes. CDOs have the knowledge and wherewithal to
help the organization along the way, but they must keep
two things in mind: the effort will be an uphill battle, and
they need buy-in and effort from others to make it happen.
The challenge of the first 100 days is still: what is the right
way to make a noticeable difference early on?

Organizations expect results from the CDO. However, it is
rare for CDOs to start with well thought out and validated
requirements. Practically speaking, getting a detailed
understanding of these data assets, and applying them in
support of strategic goals in the first 100 days is generally
beyond most CDOs' capabilities. Instead, we must be

satisfied with trying to balance general CDO output between increases in things getting better and tangible business outcomes. We mentioned this required balance in Chapter 1.

The rational approach for many organizations is integration. It is possible to produce measurable business outcomes in the first 100 days by improving integration because integration does not require hardware, software, or networks. Most often, integration demands straightforward data transformations and increased use of data standards, if there are any. If CDOs can show measurable results from an integration-based improvement, they will capture the right type of attention. But, whatever CDOs do, they must review all technology projects as soon as possible, because the project and technology cultures will conflict with a data-driven culture.

Your first 100 days

The first 100 days of a CDO's tenure are critical. Where a high percentage of new CDOs fail outright or do almost nothing, hiring executives should realize hiring the best person is only part of the equation. Newly hired leaders need support and direction to succeed. CDOs need a plan that helps them get ready to confront existing equities.

Finding a path forward in a new organization that has no established strategy seems challenging, right? It is. The first 100 days is the most crucial part of a CDO's tenure.

Triage your organization

As the saying goes, you only get one chance to make a first impression, so we encourage CDOs to plan as early as possible for their new jobs. For many, the first 100 days of a CDO's appointment are a grace period and a chance to familiarize themselves with the organization. During this time, CDOs should quickly analyze organizational dynamics and find where the power exists. They should begin to formulate an approach, make alliances, and show a caring and considerate management style that will help them cultivate new and essential relationships.

During this brief time, CDOs will make an impression on colleagues and the organization writ large. These first impressions affect a CDO's ability to baseline themselves and develop formalized plans. The CDO's early planning will help present accomplishments thoughtfully, control the message, and build alliances along the way. All this work begins with a 100-day plan.

Here are some suggestions from our own experiences:

- **Research the organization:** Learn as much as you can about the organization, its leadership, and its problems. Never go into the organization without understanding its mission and leadership.

- **Level-set your expectations:** Understand what the organization wants the CDO to do and make sure the organization understands what the CDO can do. The opposite is true too. Make sure leadership understands what a CDO brings to the organization. Marketing starts at home. So, do not be bashful. CDOs must prove their value in an up-front and honest way.

- **Be ready to preach:** CDOs are new to the organization, and the organization may not understand what the CDO is saying. So, CDOs must talk, explain, educate, and evangelize every day. CDOs must get their elevator speech ready and use it as often as they can.

- **Build relationships and build them fast:** Meet as many people as possible. Get a blend of leaders, followers, and influencers. CDOs must be sure to canvas the entire organization from operations, the C-Suite, HR, Finance, and more. A CDO will need them all.

- **Leverage existing communities:** There may already be work underway in various parts of the organization. There is little to no time to build it from scratch, so CDOs must take advantage of existing talent and insights when and where they can.

- **Name the pain:** Start making a list of organizational problems and the major pain points. CDOs must write down what they see and what people tell them. They must also avoid hearsay and speculation. Deep dives are for later.

- **Look for patterns:** Trust symmetry. CDOs must distill the crazy things people tell them in disparate conversations into cogent ideas. CDOs should look for opportunities to use the same solution in different areas. Chances are similar problems exist across the enterprise.

- **Plan, plan, and then plan:** One hundred days will go by very quickly, so CDOs should start developing a plan as soon as they can and iterate over it. Remember, data management is a program, not a project. What a CDO understands to be true one day will change the next, so CDOs must be ready to adapt and evolve.

- **Come together:** Look for opportunities to bring like-minded people together as soon as possible. This will help CDOs build a community of interest and inject some energy into their work.

- **Own the moral high ground:** People earn credibility when they work in an open and honest manner. So, CDOs must start building trust on day one. They must continue to show people that they are genuine and credible, even when things are difficult. When CDOs work this way, people will trust them, even when things get more complicated or when they face tough decisions.

- **Keep it simple:** CDOs do not have much time. They cannot solve every problem in the first 100 days. So, CDOs must be mindful of what they take on; they will have limited time to solve problems.

Avoid dis-integration

Organizations spend money, and they spend a lot on technology. However, organizations seldom evaluate technology purchases from a data perspective. Consequently, organizations pay higher costs for their technological improvements. If organizations do not include data considerations at the start, they will continue to *dis-integrate*. Dis-integration means IT systems trap data in proprietary solutions, making it extremely difficult to reuse data across the enterprise. Our research shows fewer than 1 in 10 organizations require IT vendors to supply data models as part of a technology evaluation. Ignoring data in the evaluation process produces downstream chaos and typically causes organizations to spend 20-40% of their total IT budget solving just this problem (Aiken, 2019).

CDOs can play a critical role in avoiding dis-integration. The remedy to this problem is straightforward. CDOs must be coordinating each technology purchase and make sure IT experts evaluate technology from a data perspective.

Copy from the other guy

We strongly suggest CDOs look outside their organizations for ideas and inspiration. Often, a sector may have solutions, requirements, and ideas another sector CDO can use to its advantage. The value of using ideas from another sector may not appear obvious but as discussed, the sectors are more alike than dissimilar. For example, the private sector focuses most of its resources on maximizing profits and reducing risk. Companies use their data resources to increase market control, raise public awareness, and improve the market position of its products. Meanwhile, the public sector focuses most of its resources on delivering various community services to its people. One place where private sector CDOs can use work done in the public sector is data sharing.

Increased sharing is a good thing by most accounts. But CDOs cannot blindly share data. Each sharing decision comes with a set of risks and issues. If CDOs decide sharing data is right, they must pay extra attention to something called *data pedigree*. Data pedigree uses metadata to describe a data asset and give context to it. Data pedigree is composed of two kinds of metadata: data that machines can process and data that humans can understand. People typically refer to these types of metadata as business and technical metadata. CDOs can understand how to use a data asset by asking the following kinds of questions. Taken collectively, answering these kinds of questions helps organizations make sure that they can share data in a trusted and reliable manner:

- Who produced the data?
- How is the data classified?
- What rules or laws apply to the data?
- Who manages the metadata?
- Where can organizations process and store the data?
- How reliable is the data?

Systems need technical metadata as well. Here are some questions that supply technical metadata:

- When was the data created and by what system?
- What format does the data use?
- How correct is the data?
- How complete is the data?

Knowing an asset's data pedigree helps the business protect proprietary information. Likewise, data pedigree helps governments protect government-sensitive data.

Therefore, CDOs should always consult the data pedigree to ensure everyone understands the rules for using a data asset. Similarly, CDOs must ensure the data pedigree is up to standard *before* they share it—especially if CDOs expect the recipient to follow the rules they set on the data.

An excellent example of where data pedigree is critically important is government contracting. In contracting, companies sometimes share proprietary information with the government. Companies share internal labor rates, intellectual property, and strategic business plans. If the government were not to be careful handling this kind of information, the government could injure a company causing it to lose money or go out of business. Likewise, sometimes the government shares sensitive data like plans, budgets, and national security information with companies. If companies do not consult the data pedigree for each data asset, they could mishandle a data asset and cause injury to the government.

If the government contracts with companies to deliver services, public sector authorities oversee company work, and the government has legal requirements for how the contractors should handle data. For example, the Code of Federal Regulations (CFR) describes a law called Controlled Unclassified Information (CUI), which explains the rules for handling, using, or sharing different federal data.

As a discipline, data management is still relatively new, but there is already an accepted set of principles for managing data as a strategic asset. As mentioned, DAMA has worked hard to find, organize, and promote these best practices, but organizational adoption is elusive. Other domains, however, have received help from rules. Industries such as banking and finance, transportation, and healthcare use and evolve rules and regulations. Their rules help them make informed decisions, run more efficiently, and exert better control over their organizational assets.

However, organizations are only now recognizing the need for better standards for their data. When organizations finally realize they must do something to control their costs, they often take it upon themselves to develop "standards" instead of looking to what others have already done. Public and private CDOs should examine other domains and, where proper, adopt and extend rules for their specific enterprise purposes. As thought-leader John Ladley (2010) noted, there are many domains that CDOs could consider for inspiration and adaptation:

- Physical asset management
- Supply chain management
- IT and software asset management
- Human capital management
- Financial asset management

- Records management
- Intellectual property management
- Library science

One example from author and researcher Doug Laney (2018), is the standard for fiscal management. Laney suggests that CDOs can take a tip from the set of generally accepted accounting principles (GAAP). This proven standard includes a set of principles based on financial assumptions that use a set of powerful complementary constraints. Though GAAP supplies guidelines for preparing financial information, the framework is insightful and offers a way to describe financial information and its underlying economic principles precisely.

The hard stuff is the soft stuff

The suggestions we offer are just the starting point for most CDOs. Our recommendations will not solve all the problems CDOs will meet. CDOs are on a journey of organizational change that changes all the time. CDOs must recognize they are changing culture, and that takes time. As we have said, the CDO role is still new, and organizations need time to adjust. The organization was there before the CDO arrived, and many are quite content to keep working as they have done. We encourage CDOs to work hard and carve out an area for themselves. They should focus on changing how people think about data and work hard to shape the discussion around data as being an issue for business rather than technology.

Be aware, though, CDOs are going to meet resistance somewhere. All CDOs experience pushback, so be ready for it. Be prepared to "extend the olive branch" and guide people toward constructive solutions. CDOs must be realistic too. Some organizations will not be ready for a CDO. Organizations will not assign authority or financial resources to CDOs. In these cases, CDOs will be figureheads, unable to do anything. In some rare instances, organizations will outright reject CDOs. For those in that position, do not despair. Stay calm and focus on short-term wins and do what you can.

It's getting awkward

Warning! Warning! Be ready to have uncomfortable discussions with stakeholders. When organizations get set in their ways, change is difficult. This is a common phenomenon in many organizations and well documented in academic literature. Some of the resistance manifests itself in those who have a personal stake in keeping the *status quo*. When this happens, we suggest you ask why things are the way they are. Asking *why* makes people share the rationale behind decisions. It makes them think and defend their positions. Without understanding why people do what they do, CDOs will simply be confused and frustrated. However, if you ask others to share their rationale with you, you can have a reasonable discussion on the merits of each decision.

What's in it for me?

The business case serves a valuable purpose. It helps organizations prove a value proposition and show why change is necessary. Convincing stakeholders to collaborate is not easy, however. But gaining stakeholder endorsement decreases friction and is crucial to success. Working collaboratively also proves to stakeholders that CDOs faithfully represent business interests. Therefore, the business case must use an open, transparent, and inclusive process, one designed to bring people together and share ideas and experiences. Working this way, engenders support and cooperation throughout the organization. It also results in a plan everyone supports.

But sometimes the process fails, and the programmatic documentation reflects such failure. We've seen vague and generic materials that do not sufficiently describe the organizational challenges. A good business case is measurable and actionable and should focus on a precise diagnosis of the business problems.

Digital business is placing new demands on organizations and exposing them to new threats and opportunities. Data and technology are the critical foundation, which organizations can use to meet new challenges while strengthening new business models, products, and services. To address these new demands and to reflect the growing importance of information and technology in both shaping and enabling business strategy, data leaders need to develop strategic planning skills. Leaders must understand the planning framework, the processes, the tools, and the templates needed to create, execute, and support a more integrated business and IT strategy (Cox et al., 2017).

Hobnobbing and rubbing elbows

Many organizations are responding to an increasingly digital environment by adding roles that are digitally focused or have a digital orientation (Allega et al., 2017). The list of digital roles and functions is extensive and growing. There are now digital strategists, chief digital officers, digital engagement managers, digital finance managers, digital marketing managers, digital supply chain managers, and a host of other similarly named roles. The CDO is one of these new roles. The following section offers practical advice for setting up positive and productive relationships with these common roles CDOs encounter:

- Chief Information Officer
- Chief Information Security Officer
- Privacy Officer
- Chief Archivist
- General Council
- The Legislature (Assembly or Council)
- Chief Executive (Governor, City Manager)

Chief Information Officer (CIO)

Most would agree CIOs are stretched too thin (Griffith, 2013). Organizations expect CIOs to manage internal business systems, migrate to the cloud, introduce innovations, ensure that data secure, and provide 24×7 support to global users. Ray Wang, Principal Analyst and CEO of Constellation Research Group, outlines four personas for the next-generation CIO:

- **Chief "Infrastructure" Officer**: Keeping the lights on, managing existing systems

- **Chief "Integration" Officer**: Bringing together internal and external data and systems

- **Chief "Intelligence" Officer**: Fostering business intelligence, getting the right data to the right people

- **Chief "Innovation" Officer**: Looking for disruptive technologies to drive innovation

What is clear is that CIOs give increasingly of their resources to technology and the complexity that goes with it. But what is missing here? Despite the name, CIOs pay little to no attention to data, the thing that fuels today's economies. An increased focus on data can look like the organization is adding more to the already strapped CIO's plate. We think that's far from the case.

Infrastructure

Every day, CIOs work to support systems and seem to have no money or time to do anything other than "keep the lights on." For these organizations, understanding where data lives help dictate where organizational priorities should be. One way to help set up these priorities is to determine where the most important data is. For example, as its name implies, critical systems hold important data, and the sooner organizations understand what data those systems hold, and how the organization processes that data, the sooner organizations can show the importance of that data.

After organizations review main systems, they can begin to sift through the lesser important systems to show where they can reduce maintenance costs, migrate data to other storage mechanisms, or potentially remove the systems altogether. Reducing what is needed to "keep the lights on" can yield small wins with meaningful results.

Integration

CIOs work on project-based priorities and drive results when projects are complete. The project tempo inspires their worlds—with everything having a beginning, a middle, and an end. The notion of having ongoing activities beyond staffing a help desk is rare. Sustained operations are more common on the business side of the organization, where the organization delivers services to a wide range of customers. It is here where CDOs can help CIOs with data insights. By adjusting data projects, CDOs can help CIOs manage projects through their completion. CDOs can supply insights and suggest modifications to ongoing projects to enhance the delivery of new and improved IT capabilities. Being able to help CIOs with bringing program teams together, understanding needs, helping to clarify questions about data, and integrating systems will be the most critical achievement CDOs can undertake.

Intelligence

CIOs need to shift from being project-based to performing their work with a more enterprise-wide perspective. CIOs have a long, jaded history of creating massive projects and costing organizations vast amounts of money. They buy a huge amount of equipment, hire teams of consultants, and make promises that are questionable at best. Many behave as though they have *carte blanche* when trying to change years of the business process with the latest technology promises. These efforts are rarely successful as other demands quickly eclipse the enormous effort—often resulting in financial and schedule crises. As with "keeping the lights on," understanding top organizational priorities, projects, stakeholders, and systems should always be the CDO's starting point, and, when CDOs begin their work, they should take a tip from a famous television character, Angus "Mac" MacGyver: paper clips and duct tape can only take you so far.

In contrast to CIOs, CDO roles are still new and lack the needed resources to work at an enterprise level. But this should not depress anyone; instead, it should invigorate CDOs. Not having enough resources means that CDOs should be prepared to work with paper clips, duct tape, and string. Instead of creating large programs, think about the three Ss: start by starting, show value, and set a reasonable pace for your work. Too many ideas will result in being unable to get everything implemented. Getting too many things started during the first project will leave people wanting the same or better results next time, whether you can get more resources for it or not. Pick up the pieces you can, beginning with spreadsheets and simple databases— "MacGyver it," so to speak.

Innovation

Be sure to run but run with promising ideas. Pick projects that have recognizable, urgent, and narrow issues to solve. However, always remember to start by starting, show value regularly, and set a reasonable pace for your work.

Regardless of which CIO type you work with, implementation stays a part of the CDO success plan. As they work on projects with various technical teams across the organization, CDOs meet people inside and outside their organization. Working with others presents excellent opportunities for talking about data innovation and how the CDO is instrumental in this area. In this way, change means staying ahead of the practical tasks that need completion. So, when this opportunity is available, take it.

Mark up and highlight key work areas from this book and create an elevator pitch. Having a recurring message about data and innovation related to data helps sell the idea. Gaining access to more and more diverse teams enables you to spread that message to more varied parts of the organization. Keeping an implementation mindset allows you to show practical work to the more operationally focused portions of an organization. Being ready to talk about how data innovation might affect and enable their team helps those teams see you as a strategic partner.

Chief Information Security Officer (CISO)

CISOs and CDOs share a common priority: focus on the data. Where the CDO describes the data, its sensitivity, and the rules for its usage, CISOs make sure that the organization follows the rules and that systems follow specific settings and configuration. In this way, CDOs and CISOs manage data regardless of its format, digital or analog. Continuing this comparison, CISOs are like CDOs in one crucial aspect: they should manage everything, but often only manage something. Just as data is EVERYTHING, so is security. Often is the case that, until something terrible happens, CISOs go from meeting to meeting, yelling at the tops of their lungs that the sky is falling, and it is going to hurt. In some ways, the CDO is a more recent hire and still has much ground to gain in terms of getting the budget and the understanding of real value to the organization.

Where these folks are available, learn from them. They can be staunch allies, but they can also be future tight partners. You can understand what data is out there, how to keep and use it, and your CISO will be the one to protect it. This helps the organization and allows you both to correctly complete (and keep) your jobs. On a more strategic level, the CISO also must view the organization across its entirety—the people, process, platforms, and policies. They have a high potential to be a likeminded sounding board for needed development on the enterprise level.

However, new roles mean that the likelihood of misalignment and conflict increase; therefore, it is critical organizations recognize this risk and normalize these roles as soon as possible. But saying this is easy yet preparing for a digital future is no easy task. It means data leaders must develop digital capabilities that synchronize an organization's activities, people, culture, and structure using a set of standard and ratified organizational goals.

Today, CDOs perform many of the functions that CIOs historically did. Other services, such as data analytics, are new and the role supplying these is yet undetermined. CDOs must sharpen and clarify other relationships as well. For example, CISOs manage security for IT systems and ensure IT assets follow prescribed security controls and standards. So, how do CISOs know how they should protect each data asset? The data policies tell them. And what role sets the data for each data asset? The CDO. In a way, the two roles, represent two sides of the same coin.

The CDO sets the data protection policies, and the CISO implements the security systems that satisfy those data policies. Consequently, it's not surprising the CDO and CISO must work together, develop protocols, and recordkeeping systems that keep each other informed as to what data the organization has and what the CISO must do to protect the data.

Chief Analytics Officer (CAO)

When a data analytics program exists and has matured to include elements of several parts of an organization, CAOs often manage current analytics programs and develop added measurements for organizational use and review. The CAOs are usually more technical with a background in statistics, mathematics, or engineering. They understand the algorithms used to derive insight at a deeper level than a CDO. This role must be able to communicate how to use data and under what assumptions. At the same time, the CDO is critical in supporting what is possible through governance efforts around metadata and quality.

CAOs and CDOs should work closely together. Analytic conclusions are only as good as the quality of data supporting them. The CAO must communicate data needs to the CDO, and the CDO must work on governance and its associated business processes and structures to ensure prompt, high-quality data is available for analysis. The CDO and CAO should work together to evangelize the value proposition for data. Data governance costs money, and the CAO should be able to work with the CDO to do a cost-benefit analysis showing the value of these efforts.

There are cases where CAOs do not exist in the organization, but their function is essential. The CAO plays two roles: CDO and data scientist. The CAO role can be part of the responsibilities of the CDO. Whatever the configuration, organizations must address the needs, cost, and benefits of analysis.

Privacy Officer (PO)

Like CISOs and CDOs, POs are newer roles typically within healthcare organizations. They oversee the development, implementation, maintenance of, and adherence to privacy policies and procedures about the safe use and handling of protected health information (PHI) in compliance with federal and state HIPAA regulations. As opposed to the CISO and CDO roles, there are statutory requirements for POs, which typically fall into a position within the compliance office of an organization.

While many expect the legal office to lead in this area, compliance is responsible in fact for making sure that people, processes, platforms, and policies track with the law, usually as that law is applied in audits. POs are the folks who comb through audit reports and define changes the organization needs because of inspections. Compliance is also the area expected to run efficiently and run like clockwork when no audits are happening. Consequently, studying compliance and understanding what needs they have and where they currently pull data can help you understand how easily accessible the data is. Doing this also allows you to see where data could be incrementally improved so that compliance could become even more efficient and detect problems even earlier. That's a win for everyone.

Compliance operations are different in one fundamental way: when organizations are out of compliance, regulatory agencies can assign fines and other penalties, and, because of this unique distinction, organizations tend to respond and supply enough funding to remain compliant. Though it may seem obvious, it is always easier to get something done when money, priority, and commitment exist. So, use compliance to your advantage. Tout it. Use it to your advantage to secure project funding. Exploit it to your advantage to learn more about the systems that auditors regularly inspect—RUN with it—recognized, urgent, and narrowly focused.

Chief Archivist (CA)

While library and archival knowledge have long been valued, CA positions nowadays often lack funding, although they make up a vital part of data management. In this way, the CDO and the CA are close cousins and know—unless archives or history is your business, or your organization has been sued a bunch of times for not having something required by law, and unless you work your pitch—that talking about their job at parties puts people to sleep. Archivists know where EVERYTHING is and are typically at organizations for the long-term, so they also know where all the bodies are buried, literally and figuratively.

Organizational knowledge is critical to not only know where things are but also to make sure you understand what will blow up if you try to move them. Having a mapping partner in this regard is critical because latent bombs are just waiting for you to dig them up. Many people assume archivists want to keep everything, but that is not the case. They try to understand the value of a piece of information and then properly catalog it for future use. Myths and legends about these folks are greatly exaggerated. They are valuable assets, and, when it comes to cataloging and methods for organizing, their knowledge and ability are irreplaceable.

General Counsel (GC)

Mahatma Gandhi, Nelson Mandela, and Abraham Lincoln are three men who invoke ideas of courage, integrity, and social justice. All three were attorneys; however, when one hears of lawyers today, people rarely associate honesty, courage, and fairness with them. Instead, people use words like liar, shyster, and sometimes even sleazy to describe the profession. Quick, better call Saul.

One of the most famous quotes is from William Shakespeare, who wrote, "First kill all the lawyers." What is the great bard saying about lawyers? Well, to the surprise of many, this quote means something entirely different than many would believe. In a brief 1990 *The New York Times* article (1990), author Debbie Vogel noted the line was spoken by Dick the Butcher, who wanted to disrupt the law and become king. Shakespeare's character believed that lawyers were just and too law-abiding for the menacing intent at hand. As it happens, the world has not changed that much. People often consider lawyers bad people with bad intentions merely because they raise issues and tell us a reality that is sometimes difficult to hear.

The world of technology and data has grown exponentially, not only in bytes and bits but also in terms of complexity. Today, we create and process more data than ever before, so it should not be surprising that more issues can arise than ever before. This includes legal matters.

As described, data is neutral. It is neither good nor bad. Data is simply a collection of stored facts that can describe good things or bad things. In quantitative terms, data describes the world around us. When someone creates data, the person may not be the only one affecting that data. If data is generated as part of a system, then who owns that data? Is the owner the person whose information is being entered, e.g., a citizen, or the agency that is storing that data, or the agency that may be managing the systems whereby that data is being stored?

Where people intersect is where legal analysis begins. The combinations of people and data can be staggering and determining where there is risk is not a trivial matter. The challenge for attorneys and a legal strategy exists not only in all the possibilities but also in the fact that data is rarely static, either in systems or in everyday use. In turn, legal analysis can quickly shift depending on what is happening at the time and what came first, as well as what possibilities might exist in the future. Data presents unfamiliar problems for lawyers—it is all but impossible for lawyers to list the combinatorial possibilities, legal issues, risks, and related results.

You approach your general counsel (GC) and ask, "What are the risks?" Or, "What are the legal ramifications of storing data?" Or, "How should I set retention periods?" Or, "What would happen if we sold our data?" The nature of your question is clear to you, but all they may hear is a freight train bearing down on them, whistleblowing, and headlights streaming into their faces. For attorneys, this is a terrifying predicament, and you should expect lawyers to recommend the most conservative way forward. There are just too many options, and many of them have enormous implications.

On the other hand, if CDOs operate from a strategic perspective and include counsel from the outset, GC can help the CDO gain traction, solving small but essential problems out of the gate. However, if CDOs take on too much too soon, counsel will be caught off guard and try to reign in what they perceive to be the riskiest work. So, the key to working with GC is to engage early and often. Spend time with legal counsel to understand your risks and legal requirements. Help them feel some ownership of the solutions and partnership in the decision, and GC will help the CDO gain traction—early. A good tip for finding work that would bode well for working with GC would be the "RUN" principle; distinguish work that is recognized, urgent, and narrowly focused. The combination of each of these attributes will help counsel limit exposure and reduce risk going forward.

The Legislature (Assembly or Council)

As a CDO, one of your main goals is to educate people as to the importance of data, its governance, and the tools, processes, and strategies to use data as a strategic asset. Unsurprisingly, this effort will pay dividends if your audience accepts your message. CDOs must tailor this message to the group they are trying to convince. So, CDOs should give specific thought and attention to how they communicate with the legislature. This is easier said than done because everything a CDO says becomes politically charged, no matter the intent. Nowhere are there more pronounced differences than in the legislature with its different political parties. Different constituencies, different priorities, and a stream of outside influence make working with the legislature very tricky, indeed.

Quite often, the chief executive will ban all but a few people from talking to a legislature. Usually, the CDO is under the State CIO, who supports and guides agency CIOs. Due to the excessive cost of technical resources and the many benefits of, and thus need for, technology, agency CIOs have many challenges and often insufficient resources. If your message is going to resonate, you should sell the CIO on how effort spent on data management reduces risk, improves productivity, and relieves the IT organization of work.

Visualization tools put the power of data where it should be, in the hands of business users and business decision-makers. Such tools free IT staff from writing reports. There is a flip side to this, though. For stories and insights to supply the most value, they must come from high-quality data. Data quality efforts are a joint endeavor and do require IT time, but the time is well worth it. Again, it is the CDO's responsibility to communicate and support this message.

Senior executive staff is most effective when making decisions based on high-quality data, which has context. It is the CDO's job to convey this message and secure sponsorship for data management activities. The CDO needs to communicate benefits and the required effort, including organizational change management activities necessary to set up a data-centric business. The CDO also must gauge the level of energy that is possible at the current time and craft a plan without overwhelming agency resources. The effort is well worth the time.

The legislature appropriates monies, creates positions, and conveys authority. As CDO, you must work with the legislature to explain the importance of data management. There are many challenges facing states, and high-quality data can supply the key to both reasons for the issues and workable solutions. Substance abuse, including opioid addiction, child mortality, and mass shootings, are all part of state focus. The CDO needs to work with the legislature to set up process, presence, and policy for the quality data required to solve these issues. The CDO must explain the importance of the sometimes-low-profile aspects of data management, which are vital for appropriately solving said problems.

Chief Executive (Governor, City Manager)

We save the best and the hardest for last. An understanding chief executive (Chief) can be the key to greasing all the above wheels and removing the friction that sidelines any dreams you may have about data governance and innovation. As with other stakeholders, there is the strategy and vision part of your roadshow, and then there is the proof of your implementation prowess. When you can roll up your sleeves and help solve immediate issues with exciting additions, it is easier to achieve agreement for your doing more of the same as well as potentially new projects on your roadmap.

The Chief has interests in both these outcomes. Stakeholders, constituents, and shareholders demand results, but the Chief also must be ready with all plans for "what's next." In this way, aligning your CDO goals with the Chief can prove helpful in getting those goals carried out. But, where possible, helping to implement those goals can gain a needed ally. The Chief in any organization needs the rest of the team to carry out the goals set forth. Quick and efficient implementation of one goal allows other opportunities to blossom. And when things happen for the Chief, more positive things can happen for the whole organization.

Key takeaways

- **Be transparent.** Your first 100 days are the most critical. State what you are going to do before you start doing it, or if you have already started, adjust so.

- **Get inquisitive**. Get to know people and ask many questions. If you are repeatedly asking about cursory items, then it is easier for people to understand that you are inquisitive. It may help later when you must ask the tougher questions.

- **Understand the organization.** There are many activities CDOs can undertake to get up and running quickly: know where your organization stands in relation to the data management lifecycle and know your options and how to use the ones that make the most sense for you and your organization.

- **Get data on the balance sheet.** Though many organizations seem to be on the path to good data strategy, very few truly monetize data to the extent they could and should. So, just jump in any time and see where it takes you.

CHAPTER 6

Data Planning

"Experts often possess more data than judgment."

—Colin Powell, Former Secretary of State

Data drives business. It drives operations and helps decision-makers make calculated decisions. Without data, operations stop, and leaders are left guessing. So, how can CDOs make sure they have the best data? How can they make the best decisions? The answer: treat data as a strategic asset and make it the cornerstone of organizational evolution.

Make data the cornerstone

Data is a crucial input for the creation and management of strategy and direction—regardless of its industry classification. Effective use of data requires the right decision-makers to have access to high-quality, fit-for-purpose data. This can include data from other organizations that have different charters, authority, and compliance requirements, or data from other divisions with different product offerings and reporting structures. For a comprehensive view of any business, relevant, high-quality data must be available to the proper decision-makers so they can set data policy and update and refine strategy based upon measured results and evolving challenges.

Organizations use data in a variety of ways but pay little attention to it. People just do their jobs. We ask ourselves, why? Why are many people not sensitive to what data can do for them? Why are organizations not treating data as a strategic asset? Scientists appreciate data, and there are plenty of examples of data driving new discoveries. For example, physicists using data believe they found a way to "untangle" information trapped in black holes (Mann, 2019). Other researchers believe they can prove the earth pumps liquid oxygen into its core (Letzer, 2019). No doubt, these are exciting discoveries. They capture our attention and excite us. But these are scientific examples. They are not business examples. Where can we find examples of organizations using data as a strategic asset? Here's one...

Campbell Harvey and Yan Liu (2014) study the stock market. They use data to help them understand market forces and make sound financial investments. Putting it simply, Harvey and Liu tried to make money using advanced statistics. And what do statistics need? Data. Their work may appear detailed and tedious. It might be.

But make no mistake, their research is strategic, and it could go viral. If Harvey and Liu are successful, investors could make billions of dollars using data to make financial decisions that have significantly higher returns on investment.

As we have said several times, we think data is a strategic asset, but not everyone does. People must treat data as an asset across many different business areas. According to researcher Karin Klenke, leaders still make decisions using belief systems and their gut. Until they learn something else, leaders will make decisions by the seat of their pants. So, CDOs have a special obligation to educate leaders and show them how data can help them make better decisions. If CDOs do not raise the level of decision-making, people will continue to do things as they always have—and to the detriment of everyone. CDOs must remember something when they educate people, however. They must connect high-quality data to analytics. Garbage in, garbage out.

Data's valuable, right?

Organizations keep track of things. They want to know where their valuables are. When organizations keep formal records about their assets, they call this an *inventory*. Inventories can describe material assets such as automobiles, buildings, and raw materials. But inventories can also describe intangible assets such as trademarks, customer lists, and patentable technology. Inventories can be simple, such as the number of cans of soup written on a piece of paper. Or they can be complex, like how many snowplows a state has and what their disposition is. Simply put, inventories are money. And money is a universal asset that everyone understands. So, if inventories are data, and inventories are money, does it not make sense to manage money? Of course, it does.

Because inventories are valuable, organizations often use specialized terms to describe their assets. The terms define how organizations create or purchase things, how they store items, and when they ship products to stores. In a nutshell, organizations keep track of inventory from the moment they take possession of something until they finally discard it. This timeline is known as the *product lifecycle*.

But, let's be serious. Building an inventory is not a trivial matter. Establishing a practical inventory often requires new business processes, technologies, and trained employees. When organizations finally develop a mature inventory, the system offers new insights into operational aspects of their business. For example, grocery stores keep track of products as they come and go from their stores. They know what is popular, and they know how long assorted items sit on shelves. Using this kind of information, grocery stores can stock their shelves with the most popular and profitable products. Banks do something similar. They know how much money you have, and they know who pays you. Banks can use this kind of information to sell you different financial services and lend you money.

Insatiable appetite for data

In today's networked world, data is a valuable business asset with the potential to transform every capability across the enterprise. Estimates suggest investments in business intelligence (BI) and analytics software should grow to $22.8 billion by the end of 2020 (Gartner, 2017). However, tools are not the silver bullet. People continue a disproportionate amount of time hunting for meaningful, trustworthy data, and the costs associated with searching for data are only growing. To help people at every level of the enterprise find the data they need, many organizations are considering a data catalog.

News services report the growth of data in zettabytes. This growth is unimaginable and reflects the world's insatiable appetite for data. However, despite the massive growth of data, organizations still have difficulties finding the right data. Without a systematic way to organize and use data, organizations cannot work in the modern era. But ask any technologist, and they will tell you they have the solution. Just give them the okay, and they will create an algorithm or some other technical solution that will solve the problem. We have heard stories like these for decades. And typically, leaders surrender to the technical experts. But organizations do not get the results they expect. Why is that? Leaders trusted their technical advisors and made prudent investments. The business has faster computers. It has better software, and it has smarter employees, but the business cannot get what it wants from its data. What prevents them from getting the data they need?

We believe one reason for this is because businesses do not implement reliable data management capabilities. Another key explanation involves organizations treating data as a technical issue. If the business treats data as a by-product of computing, then all later actions will not give the organization what it needs. If, however, the business treats data as a real asset—something that everyone recognizes as essential to organizational success—the business responds with ways to manage its data. For example, if the organization cannot find critical data, it sets up a system to help it discover its data. This may seem like a trivial example, but trust us, it is a big deal.

Consider this. Organizations use approximately 60% of their enterprise storage for *copy data*. This phrase describes the many copies of primary data an organization has. For example, an organization could have copies of the same data for security, testing, archives, eDiscovery, analytics, and more. Various organizational elements use copy data to help them work. For instance, IT may keep copies of data to help them recover from computing problems. Another part of the organization may keep another copy to help legal compliance, and a third part of the company may keep yet another copy to support administrative functions. What typically happens is each operational part keeps its own copy of data. And, as the number of copies multiply across an enterprise, so does the number of versions of each copy of the data. This problem magnifies as new sources of data appear. As researcher Peter Aiken notes (2016), when organizations work this way, data loses its integrity and no longer stands for the strategic assets that we need.

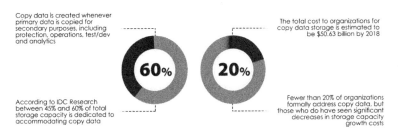

Copy data is created whenever primary data is copied for secondary purposes, including protection, operations, test/dev and analytics

The total cost to organizations for copy data storage is estimated to be $50.63 billion by 2018

According to IDC Research between 45% and 60% of total storage capacity is dedicated to accommodating copy data

Fewer than 20% of organizations formally address copy data, but those who do have seen significant decreases in storage capacity growth costs

Figure 8. Copy data problem

Aiken reminds organizations that data is different from other assets:

- **Insatiable:** data's greatest value comes people using it repeatedly.

- **Not biodegradable:** most organizational assets decay, but data improves with use.

- **Durable:** data can generate new flows of goods and services over time (Rust, 1985).

- **Strategic:** an organization must preserve data assets to achieve future outcomes.

Despite the compelling nature of data, we regularly see organizations not managing their data assets with professionalism, systems thinking, or proper technologies. If a problem involves data—and they all do—organizations always respond with a technological solution. Also, organizations regularly ignore the human dimension. Without a solid foundation in data management, organizations have no framework or policy to manage their data. They have repeatable or documented processes. The net result is a loss of organizational productivity. They spend far too much on IT investments in hardware and software without correctly implementing a data-centric means of enabling their respective knowledge workers to use and exploit data assets.

However, when you look at how organizations structure their data, one sees where data is available, you can name what information is easily accessible for use. Those elements can be a practical starting point. Years ago, data warehousing was an exciting topic for discussion until everyone realized you basically had to copy every bit of data you had to where you wanted to measure it. Short of that, what can you do? A lot.

Instead of thinking about getting a specific answer to a question, think instead about the old catalogs that used to come to your house. You could open them up and look at a section. If you had a specific need, or if you had some time in the evening or on the weekend, you could browse the whole catalog and see if there were things you needed that you did not even know existed! When organizations catalog their data, it is discoverable and available; people can gauge what they might be interested in knowing—not just a specific question they are trying to confirm. For instance, you are trying to understand how citizens consider service levels. You might try directly pulling data about wait times at service centers, or you might ask citizens to fill out a survey. Good luck getting them to take part.

Alternatively, if you only knew how many people signed on to a service and then actually used the service 20 times within the next 100 days—if you think about it, there are only two ways to discover data. In the first case, if data has been processed, it was captured by a system and is ready for the organization to use. Of course, if someone needs data from a system but is unable to access it, organizations should ensure that there is a business process in place to adjudicate access requests.

In the second case, if data has not been processed, then there is no way for anyone to retrieve it. How do people know what data the organization has? As discussed, data catalogs are the place where organizations record this kind of information. Catalogs hold information about the data assets, the stewards who control data movements, and the locations—i.e., systems—where that data lives. People may think that managing this kind of information is overwhelming and costly. We suggest the opposite. This process invokes an adage: there is never enough time to do it right the first time, but there is always enough time to do it a second time. So, take a tip from us: record this information, and develop a business process to manage it.

Bringing data together may be a headache for the CDO and team, but when data is more universally available, people may find other measures that are much easier to track and make available. Also, when data is available directly for them to consider, they are less likely to call for help on a specific answer that may or may not answer the question they want to know rather than the one right in front of them.

The experts agree

In a new book on the growing economic impact of data and analytics, IT researcher Doug Laney argues that the value of an organization's information should be on its balance sheet (Laney, 2018). By 2021, Laney predicts, many organizations will have adopted formal valuation and auditing practices for information portfolios, and stock market analysts will include outcomes like buy, hold, and sell recommendations (Laney, 2018). Today there is a burgeoning business industry built around monetizing and commercializing data. For example, some companies have business plans that call for the exclusive sale of data. That's it. That's what they sell.

In 2014, Dun & Bradstreet, a commercial data and analytics company, charged as much as $2M per year for a subscription to a data asset called the Credit Core Products and Services. As one would expect, the data asset gave subscribers access to people's credit scores. In turn, those companies could use the Dun & Bradstreet data to help make financial decisions. Dozens of other companies, like Equifax, Experian, and Trans Union, do the same thing. These companies have recognized the value of data and have developed entire businesses around its use in entirely different markets. They cleverly learned that if they manage their data, it can help others make financially-based decisions in fields such as banking, consumer lending, home lending, and automobile financing—any business that involves money lending and risk management.

Wash, rinse, and repeat

Being a CDO means being flexible, especially when you are new to the position. However, to be flexible, CDOs must adopt a customer service mentality and develop a service delivery model (SDM) for products or services for their organizations. A service delivery model is a business framework that defines the interaction between providers and consumers where the provider offers a service, whether it is information or a task. The consumer either finds value or loses value because of their interaction. An SDM has four key elements:

- Service culture
- Employee engagement
- Service quality
- Customer experience

SDMs have historically evolved from the information technology domain. Setting up an SDM starts with crafting a clearly defined mission statement and guiding principles for staff to follow. SDMs supply a set of standards, policies, and constraints to guide the designs, development, deployment, operation, and retirement of services delivered by a service (French, 2018). Data management services do not magically appear. CDOs produce them. CDOs organize deliver services like data processing, cataloging, and archiving, to their organizations. CDOs must incorporate SDMs as part of their operational plans. Without an SDM, CDOs would have offerings that consumers would not trust. For example, deliveries could be one-off solutions when consumers expect repeatable or continuous deliveries.

CHAPTER 7

Culture Eats Data for Breakfast

"An organization's ability to learn, and translate that learning into action rapidly, is the ultimate competitive advantage."

—Charles Dickens, Author

There are no unicorns, no magic potions, and no easy solutions to become a successful CDO. We know, too, that changing organizations is immensely tricky (Aiken and Harbour, 2017). In practical terms, the first CDO hired will likely incur organizational resistance fueled by deeply rooted culture, tradition, and institutionalized control issues that can destroy the CDO. We have seen this happen many times, and it continues today. Knowing this, the first CDO must be a risk-taker and be able to move fast.

The CDO must be able to quickly develop a data strategy and align it with an organizational strategy. The CDO must also quickly earn the trust of stakeholders across the entire organization. Working too slow in both areas will prove fatal to the CDO.

CDOs must also master communications and organizational change management. If a CDO's organization does not currently have this ability, find it, fast. For change management, the range of culture is not as important as its size. Organizations grow in ways that attract folks who want to work "like this" and who balance characteristics such as work-life similarly. Culture can work directly for you or against you, but do not leave this critical outcome to chance.

Fix the real problems

Center on the problem and engage business professionals on the availability of data sources that can be used to solve the problem. Much like a programmer trying to understand a business practice by asking questions to build a conceptual model, your lack of business understanding can be an asset in this phase. People will be more willing to ask and challenge the business data stewards and current business owners, even engage them to think about the problem in a new manner, while they are finding answers to your questions.

Start by asking for a description of the problem and solutions that can be used to tackle it. Add to the strategy; even if it seems naïve, you show interest, and you might even stumble on to a plan. Ask about what data sources would be relevant to the solution, and if data is used to drive any strategy.

If data is available to start using it, confirm the inferences currently at play and the strategy, if possible. Visualization tools can be great for this also. If you have the technical acumen or people on your staff that do, there are many open-source tools for analytics that can be employed to both test the strategy and supply evidence for the cause of the issue.

If you do not have the technical capabilities, using university relationships can be useful. Many graduate programs are looking for data issues to tackle, and the key for these students and professors is access to high-quality data. Students and professors will also question the domain and the approach and confirm strategies. As they are both outside the field and experts on machine learning, their suggestions will reinforce your messages, especially about data quality. Also, as these are research efforts, exceptions such as those in the Family Educational Rights and Privacy Act (FERPA) might apply in this context and no other settings.

Data quality is key to good analytic outcomes. If the data cannot be relied on, either during training or execution, then the results themselves will be unreliable (Carlton et al., 2018). Working with existing data sources and looking at the critical dimensions of data quality against these sources juxtaposed with the quality of inference about the data can be a powerful exercise to drive the message of the importance of high-quality data in decision making (Satterfield, 2015). Again, visualization tools can be beneficial for showing trends before and after applying data quality improvements. This exercise also explains how you can be responsive more quickly than expected according to the standard timeframes of state government.

Incorporate other data sources to solve the problem. Of course, some data sources might not be available. If this is the case, you face an excellent opportunity to review the current process for data sharing. Further, you have the opportunity to standardize the request and structure of agreements to hasten the sharing process and ensure sharing in compliance with established rules. This also supplies an opportunity to show where agencies can cooperate on other problems by sharing data and efforts.

Data sharing discussions can motivate discussions about the importance of reference data, master data, and metadata—especially as related to data pedigree. Data quality efforts can reveal issues in data for which standard repositories exist. Reference data repositories can exist internally or externally, and this is an opportunity to advocate for their use. Working with other agencies on usual problems can show where common data is and help drive master data management to reduce duplicate data. Discussions addressing data sharing also motivate conversations related to the importance of data lineage to ensure that applicable compliance and security concerns are addressed. These efforts make a compelling case for a data management framework that supports both local needs and the enterprise vision.

Where does it hurt most?

How do organizations begin this transformation? Where do they start? Our answer to these big questions is simple: where does it hurt the most? The answer to this question gives rise to others. Where does the organization have a problem that needs immediate attention? What is a real and lingering problem at your organization, and how can data management affect a positive outcome?

Once you know what you want to solve, you can do what we just did—look at where it may have started and what is causing it. This is known in some circles as root cause analysis. It sounds complicated, but it is straightforward. Pick a problem and begin asking many questions.

For instance, with our example above, why do business leaders view all issues and processes as a technology issue in need of a solution? Answer: Because business leaders do not always understand what technology can and cannot do, they know what they want to achieve as a business, which does not always translate to technology. Why do business leaders not understand technology, and still struggle with explaining their needs to technology? Answer: Because, even though more technology leaders are in businesses, technology is always driven by budget. And budgets still limit technology changes to mostly incremental changes rather than broader implementations. Why do technology changes only happen incrementally? Answer: Because they are usually more expensive since they occur gradually, and, often, smaller changes result in unforeseen consequences when business shifts again later.

As we move along each step of this root cause analysis, a few opportunities arise. We get a clearer understanding of the issue at hand without necessarily pointing the finger at a party. We also start seeing opportunities for improvement. For instance, if IT knew where the business wanted to go in the future, different choices may be available when implementing short-term fixes to help the company in the immediate term. We also see that, if IT understood the impact of changing a portion of the system for one business need, one might be able to see where even small changes might impact future development.

How does this work in the current world? Sometimes the CDO needs to come in and merely start asking many questions. You may get input about these questions from a variety of stakeholders and organizational leaders. Of course, it may take some time to bring all forces together to make sense of where the genuine issues lie.

But some organizations have been able to charter the CDO with problems in mind. For example, Indiana has had success with analytics and the ability to show causal relationships for fighting infant mortality. Florida has worked hard to supply open data to its citizens to increase governmental transparency and support entrepreneurial efforts and innovation. Virginia has specifically called up experts to work on the opioid crisis and substance abuse in the creation of its CDO position. Working these kinds of problems imbues political capital to leadership and serves as a platform from which the CDO can show good data management in direct support of political priorities.

Either way, it can be exciting! With the first, the CDO gets to help the organization chart its course and issues for priority, but this can often take extra time to gain alignment. With the second, the organization may set a path that helps gain footing; but the road may change— sometimes rather quickly, so it is important to consider root cause analysis always—even when the path is set, just in case you must shift soon.

Seems overwhelming? Take heart. The second most-often listed definition of "digital business" is "using data to manage better business performance," picked by 49 percent of those surveyed. It turns out that organizations understand they must use data and that it can help them; they need someone to prove how to do it.

Where did I put those stakeholders?

Many data management programs struggle to achieve and sustain business engagement because the organization either sees no business value or misses the opportunity to lead a large change effort.

If you want to move forward, you need greater business engagement because only the business can supply a holistic view of its priorities. The multistep process can create measurable indicators of what success looks like at a business process or strategy level. Again, only the business can determine such a view and enable you to quantify the business benefits of the data management program in financial terms. Business cases and metrics are more than mere "speed bumps" to be passed at the beginning of the program and never revisited. Instead, these factors are a critical reference point for stakeholders until circumstances change.

Councils set up by states are a wonderful place to start. Not only do they articulate a sponsored mission and principles, but they are results-driven as well. Many times, such councils also receive help from universities and non-profit organizations. Non-profits support funding and public domain research, which can engender trust, help buy-in, and supply guidance as to where to start solving problems.

Talking with your legislature or executive governing body and reviewing political positions and promises is also a reliable source of direction in determining a challenge on which to work. This gains buy-in and shows that the promises can be fulfilled. It also allows the legislature to claim innovation and responsiveness as the problem gets solved, especially if a coalition can be formed and if an innovative and cost-effective approach can be used.

Look for local opportunities where you can be a bridge to state agencies. There are many local efforts to use data, from child welfare to law enforcement. These activities help local communities and supply opportunities for the CDO to set up the ability to be a coordinating force. It is important—*in all* efforts—that you stand for value-added and take what is given; trust takes time to prove.

Businesses need high-quality data for effective decision-making across multiple layers of any organization. Those decisions must rely on trustworthy data to show the most effective strategies for implementing the organizational vision. And the same requirement exists at the business steward and business owner levels responsible for ensuring data quality and data governance fidelity with business goals.

Be sure to understand who the stakeholders are. Get them involved and help them get skin in the game. Be sure to listen to their ideas before giving your opinion.

Understand their perspective on issues and resist the urge to tell them that you have all the answers to their problems. Instead, CDOs should carefully communicate ideas without threatening the existing bureaucratic base. They should focus on listening, then use learned information to persuade stakeholders to take ownership of distinct parts of the problem and reshape the organization in ways that align with the desired outcome rather than the CDO's ideas and goals.

Learn how stakeholders can become part of your movement. And, most of all, help them rally around desired outcomes instead of specific methods, tools, or techniques. For example, if you want to develop a data management policy for your organization, keep it at a high level. Prepare the plan to avoid controversy. If you do this, others across the organization who read the plan will not detect threats to their existing power base. Get buy-in at this level first, then develop a companion process that describes the business steps that the organization should follow to satisfy the policy. Walking in a stepwise progression allows you to create small wins, easily tie in with existing efforts, and bring others along without having to drag them. People are more likely to work with you when they can walk slowly rather than having to sprint to keep up with you.

After CDOs secure stakeholder confidence, stakeholders can act as a force multiplier for making other changes across the organization. Stakeholders become strategic allies for CDOs as they grapple with new and unfamiliar problems and help shape solutions. Stakeholders can also help win the hearts and minds of others across the organization. Remember, CDOs must build a movement for change, and it is essential CDOs bring others along with them. We recommend CDOs use their authority sparingly. Instead, CDOs should help people better understand the goals the existing order sets for its data and its use.

CDOs are often new to many organizations. To break through this barrier, CDOs must find ways to get stakeholder support as soon as possible. If CDOs do not get stakeholder endorsement, CDOs will meet entrenched bureaucrats who try to "wait the guy out." Make no mistake. This is hard to do. If CDOs are not successful, others may take matters into their own hands and put someone else in the job. Then it is business as usual. So, we suggest CDOs work hard developing a strong stakeholder network and exercise team building, collaboration, and communication skills at every step.

Partner with IT

Similarly, when you finish this work, then—and only then—should CDOs attempt to step into the standards world. CDOs must recognize that IT excels at setting technical standards. This is where CDOs will meet the most significant resistance. However, this is also where CDOs can most easily garner IT support. Why? Because the CDO has addressed and solved the business problems without "rocking the boat." The CDO has focused on the outcome and not on the technical solution. When CDOs reach this level, they should celebrate their success and ask IT for help developing professional standards. Setting technical standards is one of the things that IT does best, so create that alliance and get ITs help.

Recognize, too, that there are many kinds of stakeholders. They exist across the organization at all levels, including the executive suite, but they not limited to these general levels. Sometimes the folks outside of the executive suite know more about how the detailed work is done. In one part of the organization, stakeholders may be managers; in other parts, they may be businesspeople, and, still, in other areas, they may be executives. Each of these roles has a different and crucial organizational perspective that CDOs should address. The last thing CDOs need is to overlook a key stakeholder only to learn later that an individual could have helped the CDO overcome a tough hurdle. So, be sure to show everyone and update your stakeholder list often; people come and go all the time.

One of the most critical stakeholders is the CDO's champion. This person is an individual who supports the CDO. Without this person's support, organizations will not be able to use the CDOs and change the organization way they want. Ideally, CDOs would have many heroes, but it can be difficult to find allies initially. You can start without a champion, but if you are supposed to make organizational changes, you must find the support. More than one champion is always better, given the high turnover rates for members of executive teams.

Just the facts Ma'am

Guiding people in new directions can happen in many ways. When you go in new directions that people have not seen before, show them. Gather examples of good data management and governance from the private and public sectors alike. Indeed, CDOs can receive some real benefits from showing where others have gone before, but, like any good envisioning exercise, it is much easier to get "there" when you know what "there" looks like.

On the other hand, many people can look at the same object and see quite different things. So, showing people examples comes with some context-setting suggestions. For instance, what and how you present your evidence of "good" data management can affect people's understanding based on several factors:

- Data maturity of your stakeholders
- Willingness of transparency and collegiality of your stakeholders

- Understanding of and receptiveness to change and risk
- Solution timeline
- Sharing of evidence available to motivate an audience to continue working on a problem
- How solved the problem needs to be at various stages of the effort

As with other recommendations in this book, consider your audience. Get to know the people you must speak with—not just who they are, but how they think, work, and assimilate the latest information. Planning for such conversations can help you adjust your presentation to fit your audience. Fortunately, there are so many notable examples of good data management; peppering them in at the right times with the right audience can help spice up the conversation—but not make them sneeze at a whiff of change.

Follow the Yellow Brick Road

Data lifecycle management (DLM) describes and verifies business processes for data asset requirements. What data does the organization need? When do they need it? And what formats does information technology need? In a sense, data lifecycle management is the yellow brick road leading to Oz. DLM helps ensure organizations follow best practices from the moment data originates through its final disposition. Taken together, these best practices make up the DLM function. Also, DLM intends to meet and exceed the information needs of all enterprise stakeholders in terms of information availability, security, and quality. Other DLM goals include:

- Capturing, storing, protecting, and ensuring the integrity of data assets
- Continually improving the quality of data and information
- Ensuring privacy and confidentiality and preventing unauthorized or inappropriate use of data and information
- Maximizing effective use and value of data and information assets

DLM begins at creation or acquisition for each data asset and continues throughout their useful life to their eventual archiving or destruction. Along the way, the organization monitors data. Also, the organization scopes each data asset to prioritize and align each one with core business goals through the data management strategy.

Data lifecycle phases include the following six elements:

- Business direction (data requirements, creation, acquisition)
- Development (architecture, design)
- Implementation (physical architecture)

- Deployment (insertion into the operational environment)
- Operations (data transformations, usage, performance, and maintenance)
- Disposition (destruction and archiving)

Effective DLM depends on the definition and documentation of key business processes integral to organization-wide functions and business systems. The business must define and ensure each business process is within scope. Once data assets have been initially mapped, the business must confirm and approve process owners for each data asset.

Key takeaways

- **Ask questions**. Learn what the real data problems are instead of solving perceived problems.

- **Find educational partners**. Schools seek real-world problems, and CDOs have opportunities to get extra help.

- **Start solving the most important problems first**. Understand where your organization's biggest problems are. Tackle them before other problems.

CHAPTER 8

Your Assets are on the Line

"It is a capital mistake to theorize before one has data."

—Sherlock Holmes (Sir Arthur Conan Doyle)

Okay, be honest. Do you know what data your organization has? Probably not, and this is a real problem. Maybe you wanted to get a correct accounting for some time but, for a million different reasons, things did not progress. We find this to be a pretty familiar story among CDOs. So, why are most organizations in this position? We all say that data is valuable. We all say that data is critical to developing insights and running our businesses. Then why is it so difficult to answer the foundational question, "what data do you have?"

Part of the answer relates to the fact that keeping a list of data assets is hard. We know that it is not sexy work. We know that sometimes it can be tedious. We also know that this is not what many people want to do, but, again, be honest. Without knowing what data your organization has, how can you take on more complex work like integrating data or doing analytics at scale? Without first understanding what evidence you have and what rules apply to it, you are going to find yourself unable to advance the way that you want. So, what can you do about it? Let's take a look.

The first step toward setting up data as an asset is giving it the respect it deserves. Think about it for a moment. We expect every modern organization to have an exact and complete account of staff. We know when they joined an organization, we know when they left, we know what positions those people hold, and we know how much money we pay them. We know a tremendous amount of information about our people. However, we spend little time thinking about those same human resource systems that amass the data we are collecting.

We know what people we have, where they are, and what they do. This is an impressive amount of information. Why is that? Why are we willing to put considerable resources behind knowing this amount of information about our people? Most would agree people are the most valuable asset that any organization has, and we must understand a lot about those assets to run our organizations. We understand that people are the cornerstones of our organizations.

But as our organization becomes more dependent on data, we must adjust our strategic thinking and treat data like we treat people. For example, how do we know how much money we pay? Data. How do we know who works for whom? Data. How do we know what someone does for the organization? Data.

Organizations have become wholly dependent on data without which the most basic questions cannot be answered. What data do you have? And where is it? And what are people doing with it? When we recognize that information is a cornerstone of organizations, then we can begin to move our organizations in the direction we wish to go.

As Norm used to say: Measure twice

The business environment constantly changes. Laws change, relationships change, and people change. In the private sector, customers keep organizations in business. In the public sector, the government, the public, medical patients, and other stakeholders supply resources allowing the government to continue to supply public services (Johnson, 2011). However, the environment threatens those same organizations. Volatile shifts in market demand, new regulatory requirements, disruptive technologies, or the entry of new competitors, can easily affect the environment and those organizations working within it. Some of these environmental forces can affect public sector organizations, as well.

The environment affects everything, and in this way, public and private sector organizations are equivalent. The environment can help or hinder either. For some, the environment can supply opportunity and success, but the environment can also be fatal for other organizations not understanding the forces in play. Therefore, organizations must be on guard and constantly analyze environmental forces and decide which affects them. Several stages make up an environmental analysis. Sometimes known as the *discovery, assessment,* and *current state,* this sort of analysis supplies a snapshot or a coarse understanding of an organization's ecosystem and what forces could affect it (Nichols, 2015).

When performing an environmental assessment, organizations survey their business goals, existing information, competitive position, operations, and governance structures. This type of analysis generates a detailed description of the environment and helps leaders understand how they would perform under different environmental conditions. Understanding how the organization responds to different environmental conditions helps the organization develop various operational models ahead of changing environmental conditions. For example, organizations can find functional gaps, issues, pain points, strengths, and other requirements. Business strategists use this information to determine how the organization should change.

A framework designed specifically to help organizations perform environmental assessments and understand how well they manage their data is the Data Management Maturity Model (DMM). The DMM is a comprehensive reference model for state-of-the-practice process improvement. The DMM defines the fundamental business processes of data management and specific capabilities that constitute a graduated path to maturity. It allows organizations to evaluate themselves against documented best practices, determine gaps, and improve the management of data assets across functions, lines of business, and geographic boundaries (Carnegie Mellon University, 2014).

When organizations evaluate foundational data management capabilities, which are prerequisites to more advanced data capabilities such as data mining, master data management, or data warehousing, the model can help. The DMM provides a framework for use when assessing the organization's ability to develop improved data management practices around the core disciplines of data: data management strategy, data quality, data governance, data platform and architecture, and data operations (Carnegie Mellon University, 2014).

When an organization performs a data maturity assessment, the performance of each practice area is compared to public standards. The DMM helps practitioners and executives understand not only how well the organization performs work, but also what the organization still needs to do. Measuring organizational performance illustrates status and shows the need for planning for improvements as they strive for world-class data management practices. The framework further supports the objective measurement of progress compared to discrete data management functions and abilities.

STRATEGY

Best practices for establishing, communicating, justifying, and funding a collaborative vision for data management.

GOVERNANCE

Best practices for ensuring broad participation in the practice and senior oversight of the effectiveness of data management.

OPERATIONS

Best practices for specifying data requirements and managing implemented data across the entire supply chain.

ARCHITECTURE

Best practices for establishing methods and standards that successfully integrates archives, and retains data assets.

QUALITY

Best practices for defining and implementing a collaborative approach for detecting, assessing, and cleansing data defects.

Figure 9. DMM practice areas

The DMM focuses attention on organizational data maturity across five aspects:

- **Data Management Strategy.** Defines the vision, goals, and aims for the data management program. The strategy also ensures that stakeholders and priorities are in alignment.

- **Data Quality.** Encompasses process areas designed to provide the means for an organization to fully understand the nature and quality of the data under management, as well as mechanisms to evaluate, prevent, and remediate defects to assure that the class of data meets business purposes and the organization's strategic objectives.

- **Data Governance.** Addresses the processes that help collaborative decision-making to implement the building, sustaining, and compliance functions of governance bodies.

- **Data Platform and Architecture.** Encompasses process areas designed to create the optimal data framework to meet present and future business objectives; establish and implement well-crafted, enforceable standards; select a platform and supporting technologies that meet scope and performance requirements; integrate disparate sources of data; and manage historical and aged data effectively.

- **Data Operations.** Encompasses process areas designed to provide the means for an organization to fully understand the nature and quality of the data under management and mechanisms to evaluate, prevent, and remediate defects to assure that the class of data meets business purposes and the organization's strategic objectives.

Assessors rank organizational performance using the following rating system.

1. **Performed.** The organization performs processes on an *ad hoc* basis, primarily at the project level. The organization typically does not apply consistent processes across business areas. For the most part, process discipline is reactive. For example, data quality processes emphasize repair over prevention. The organization makes foundational improvements but limits its gains to a single business area and not the enterprise.

2. **Managed.** The organization plans and executes policy using defined processes, skilled workers with adequate resources to produce controlled outputs are employed, relevant stakeholders are involved, and the organization monitors activities for adherence to the defined processes.

3. **Defined.** A set of standard methods is employed and consistently followed. The organization tailors

its processes to meet specific needs that distinguish them from the set of conventional procedures according to the organization's guidelines.

4. **Measured**. Vetted process metrics are in use for data management. Such metrics include control of variance, prediction, and analysis using statistical and other quantitative techniques. The organization manages its performance processes across the life of the process.

5. **Optimized**. The organization perfects its performance processes with the application of analytical results from Level 4, leading to targeted improvement. The organization shares its best practices with peers and industry.

Systems like the DMM are excellent tools to inform strategy, and governance is the tool organizations use to implement strategy and set corporate direction. The goal of data governance is not just to clarify who 'owns' data but also to position data to perfect its value. Data is the resource an organization uses to improve business performance; however, organizations can't use all their data. Some data is not in a ready state and could introduce more problems. Accordingly, the responsibility for data governance efforts should fall at least as much on business as it does on IT—preferably more. CIOs are overwhelmed. Change happens so fast that it is a full-time job to keep up with technology. The result? Data suffers, as well as the business processes that support it. This means that CDOs must stay focused on the data while the CIOs stay focused on the technology.

Lists are your friends

A catalog systematically organizes things using lists that have descriptive details. Also, catalogs record information describing data. A data inventory consists of two types of information: 1) human-readable and 2) machine-readable. Human-readable information includes details like data origination, usage terms and conditions, and data classification. A catalog has machine-readable information like data asset size, its creation date, and modification date. A catalog also includes other information that helps users understand the meaning of a data asset. Examples of this information include semantic models, data type definitions (DTDs), or other documentation that aids users in assessing the relevance of a data asset for analytical or administrative work.

Additionally, organizations want to know other things about their data. For example, where is it? Whom should I contact to get a copy of it? Is it okay for me to use that data where I want to use it? And what can I do with the data? These are all great questions. So, it follows that your data catalog would also hold information about the location of each data asset. For instance, you might be able to learn that information describing corporate sales is in the organization's customer resource management (CRM) system. Similarly, you might be able to learn that you could use that data for an analytic purpose, but you might also discover that before you are allowed to use it, that you must limit the sharing of that data only to people who have the authorization to access that data (dissemination controls). You might also learn that the organization must use specific data in technical environments that have required restrictions.

Be ready to think through the kinds of things that you want and must know about your data. Think about all the scenarios that would allow you to safely and effectively discover, request, process, exploit, and dispose of your data. Then, realize that you must know a lot about your data assets. However, when you have an established data catalog, recognize that you can save an enormous amount of time and labor solving the most straightforward problems. Now you are ready to take on your organization's big issues in a new way.

When do you inventory data?

Defining data catalogs can be complicated. Let's start with what they are not. In a word, they are not projects. What do we mean? We mean that keeping track of your assets is not a one-and-done effort. Instead, keeping track of your data—from the moment it exists until you dispose of it—is an ongoing effort that ends when your organization no longer needs specific data. As we mentioned, you should think of your data catalog the same way you do about your HR system. Your HR system has an inventory of your people assets, and the data catalog includes a list of your data assets. So, dispel the idea that you can design, build, and populate your data catalog in a few weeks (as some vendors have assured you). Instead, start thinking that managing your data catalog is part of how you do business.

How do you build a data inventory?

Who builds and keeps the data catalog? Who are the people that will comb through the organization looking for data that should be in your inventory? Chances are you already have some people, but you might not have them all. Think of it this way: who records information about your organization's people? In most organizations, HR does that work. HR already records a tremendous amount of information about your employees.

Who records information about your IT infrastructure? In most organizations, IT does that work. They know all the information about technology resources, their physical location, who manages the machinery, and who administers the computing resources. Okay. That makes sense too.

Who is the authority about how the computing resources must be configured and controlled? Again, in most organizations these days, information security does that work. The business experts are the people that determine the relative sensitivity of each data asset. The business decides what the organization does with its data.

If you stop and think about what your organizations already do, you realize that your data catalog is the aggregation of information you are already collecting. Instead of using the HR data to administer benefits and salaries, the data catalog would use some of that same information to describe users and consumers of a data asset. Instead of using IT information to schedule the next system backup, the data catalog would use some of that information to understand what IT systems hold a data asset. And instead of information security guessing as to the sensitivity of a data asset, the data catalog would inform information security as to how they should protect that asset in any IT system. Thinking of things in this way radically changes your view of the work necessary to build and keep a data catalog. Where you might assume that your organization needs a small army of catalogers, the problem becomes one of system integration and the management of data that you already collect. However, there are things that these groups do not do, and for that work, we need some new experts.

Even though machines do some remarkable things, they do not know any information that is outside the system, and, for this work, organizations need experts to record— at least one time—*information that the system can use to automate dozens and even hundreds of downstream processes.*

Describing data assets

Being able to use data effectively hangs on your ability to describe data assets in a way that works for the entire organization. As we know, not everyone describes things the same way. Therefore, when we describe our data assets, we must consider using terms and descriptors that are meaningful and relevant to different kinds of consumers like businesspeople, IT specialists, legal staff, and data analysts. These people all describe data differently, so it is essential to recognize the distinction and make sure that your data catalog serves the needs of them all. At its core, we are talking about documenting your data holdings in ways that explain how the organization created data, what the data means, their content and structure, and any data manipulations that might have taken place. CDOs should consider following best practices when creating, organizing, and managing data. The data architecture and attendant business glossary are vital for long term data preservation. Together, these descriptors supply people with contextual information that they need to make sense of that data (Vanden & Eynden, 2011).

Specifically, good data documentation includes information about the following aspects:

- **Data collection context**: project history, aim, goals, and hypotheses.

- **Data collection methods**: sampling, data collection process, instruments used, hardware and software used, scale and resolution, temporal and geographic coverage, and secondary data sources.

- **Dataset structure**: data file pedigree and lineage, study cases, relationships between files, data validation, data checking, proofing, data cleansing, quality assurance procedures, carried out changes made to data over time since original creation, and identification of different versions of data files.

- **Data protection**: access and use conditions rules, and data confidentiality rules.

Data files have self-describing information. Many data analysis software packages have facilities for data annotation and classification employing variable attributes—labels, codes, data type, or missing values, for example—data type definitions, table relationships, and more. Other documentation may be contained in publications, final reports, working papers, and lab books or created as a data collection user's guide. At the data-level, documentation may include these more descriptive distinguishing factors:

- Names, labels, and descriptions for variables, records, and their values
- Explanation or definition of codes and classification schemes used
- Definitions of specialist terminology or acronyms used
- Codes of, and reasons for, missing values
- Derived data created after collection, with code, algorithm, or command file weighting, and grossing variables created
- Data listing of annotations for cases, individuals, or items

These descriptors, known as preservation metadata, are essential because digital objects are technology dependent. Unlike printed books or oil paintings, users cannot "directly" access the contents of digital objects; instead, a complex technological environment, consisting of software, hardware, and, in some cases, network technology, sits between the user and the object's contents. Rendering and using digital objects requires the availability of this environment—or at least some technically equivalent substitute. For this reason, it is insufficient to preserve a digital object; systems must make and use the objects as well.

Rendering objects on-demand is non-trivial. Technology changes very rapidly, and if organizations do not support this information, the data quickly becomes unintelligible and of no value to the organization. Consequently, it is especially important to carefully document the technical environment of an archived digital object to ensure it remains usable for current and future generations (Lavoie, 2005).

Leveraging your data catalog

Many organizations implement data governance without knowing what data they have. Those same organizations develop rules and issue orders without understanding what data they affect and what the consequences are to their organizations. This may seem odd at first, but it happens. We recommend organizations implement data governance while simultaneously creating a data catalog. By develop catalogs and governance at the same time, organizations can use their data catalogs and use them as a reference for knowing what policies apply to which data assets. For example, when your organization names a data asset, the organization can also record the policy decision in your data catalog, thereby becoming another piece of information that supplies context for future uses of that same data asset. In this fashion, your organization can introduce a new level of consistency about data, its use, and even legal and regulatory compliance.

Notably, organizations react in response to adverse events. For example, it is typical for organizations to start cataloging data on the heels of a data breach or spill rather than make a deliberate effort to use data holdings more effectively and efficiently. Typically, after some time, these same inventories receive insufficient support and fall into decay until the next crisis. Forward-looking organizations, however, realize they can increase the value of their data by using data catalogs and using them to support other functions, such as security, business development, regulatory compliance, or analytics. Using data catalogs in this manner results in an official ledger of nearly every aspect of the organization's data: usage terms and conditions, people and systems authorized to access data, and decisions made by various organizational authorities to guide the distribution, dissemination, release, and disposition of data.

By using data catalogs, enterprises can use the inventory to not only understand their data holdings, but also to begin the elimination of unnecessary caches of redundant, obsolete, and trivial data. Regularly reviewing data inventories will help organizations focus and pare information, limit access to only those with an actual business need, and even get rid of data entirely. Equally important, catalogs help regulate the sharing of data based on the examination and evaluation of each data sharing request. Catalogs help the discovery of opportunities to limit the type and amount of data organizations share and by placing more privacy controls around processes (Wachs, 2015). Organizations can also use data catalogs as a toolset to control all activities across the entire data lifecycle. Such leverage supplies instant access to all decisions about the approved disposition of data.

Controlling costs with a data inventory

The impact of digital information has been remarkably universal, extending to industry, government, and academia; to businesspeople, scientists, engineers, and scholars of the humanities; to the individual in the workplace and the individual in the home (Lavoie, 2014).

Organizations produce, use, and share vast quantities of information in digital form for many purposes. Their ability to create and consume digital information has steadily progressed, and with new and exciting advances, it must be ensured that people are using the data appropriately such that, thanks to good stewardship, the data will be usable in the future. However, long term data preservation comes with costs. The organization must consciously commit to making sure that data is ready when the organization needs to use it. Having data in a ready state means that leadership assigns responsibility to the data leader, incentivizes people to raise data quality, and assigns costs to the proper organizational elements.

Just as the benefits of data transcend individuals, systems, and specialties, so do the challenges which organize them.

The heart of data governance

Organizations have been talking about data governance for quite some time, but few have shown that they understand what it takes to do it. Data governance is starting to expand beyond the traditional regulatory requirements—for risk and cost control—into ways organizations can drive business value. Data governance is a crucial part of this strategy, through specifying policies overseeing data; guaranteeing that data policy, standards, and procedures are seen; and operationalizing processes in a trustworthy, reliable, and auditable manner. Shrewd CDOs establish an organization's data governance program, get the right technologies to support it, and assemble the right team to establish data governance across the organization.

CDOs must recognize, however, that data governance and IT governance often become intertwined. Tangling data and IT governance leads to confusion and detracts from the enterprise value of the data portfolio, further leading to ineffective data practices, increased risks to data, and confusion over data authorities. CDOs should remember that data governance enables the successful business architecture, recording, and use of data assets to drive better intelligence decisions and, ultimately, achieve strategic outcomes.

What does data governance entail, and how does an organized program go beyond traditional data management processes and procedures? An organization's data management activities—such as archiving, backup and recovery, system security, and data disposition—may already adhere to proven policies. However, a data governance program is meant to *create an ongoing practice to coordinate the definition of policies and standards and enforce their compliance.* A data governance program encompasses the organizational structure, such as a data governance council and affiliated data stewards and analysts, an operating model within which those parties work together, and defined procedures that guide their activities. The goals for setting up data governance include:

- To define and agree on data policies, standards, and rules that govern across the data lifecycle
- To develop procedures for operationalizing compliance with policies and standards and put those procedures into production
- To continuously check compliance and act when necessary

North to Alaska

While increasingly CDOs are talking about data governance, they should also realize that governance is technically complex, organizationally challenging, and politically sensitive. Besides, securing executive-level sponsorship for governance programs is challenging because, in general, business leaders do not recognize the need for governance. Lack of data appreciation among business leaders is starting to change, however, as executives realize that the solutions to many business problems—such as regulatory compliance, reduced litigation costs, and decision-making transparency—are grounded in good data management practices.

What often happens, though, is data governance often lands, by default, in the hands of IT. Unfortunately, when organizations define data as a byproduct of IT, the landscape changes entirely: no longer is data a business asset; it is simply the goal of a computing challenge and treated like other IT assets. Technology is a marvelous thing, and we support it wholeheartedly. However, CDOs must separate business problems and technology problems. So, if data is only as valuable as the business processes, decisions, and interactions it enables and improves, it MUST remain a business asset, one for which business takes the decisions concerning its acquisition, use, and final disposition. The ultimate goal of data governance is to generate the highest possible return on data assets. If a business wants to be sure it captures critical opportunities to use data to support operations, strategy, and customer experience, it needs to govern data assets as it does other enterprise assets, such as financial securities, cash, or HR.

In this way, data governance must fill the same sort of role as finance and HR: a coordinated enterprise effort that protects and perfects the business value of the organization's assets, including its data assets. As with other business functions, people, policies, and processes, the CDO must measure the success, compliance, and organizational effectiveness of data governance initiatives. Data governance and the supporting data stewardship processes rely on technologies such as data integration, data quality, master data management, metadata management, data masking, data security, data archiving, and BI software. But business needs should drive the process and use technologies to support those needs.

More organizations are hiring CDOs and forming data governance bodies to set up data policies that promote data quality and usability when they recognize that data governance is a priority. However, implementing data governance can be complicated, confusing, and frustrating. Programs that focus only on organizational structure and operating models or try to survey data structure and semantics from the bottom-up may need more support to develop the socialization, championship, and resources required to ensure sustainability.

Because today's organizational data environments are involved, corporate teams must manage many systems and platforms for transaction processing, operational processing, BI, reporting, and analytics. Some organizations cope with the growing complexity by implementing practices to organize, manage, and govern the use of data assets across business functions and technological boundaries.

Leading the way

The reward structure, the organizational climate, and the work structure can change, but usually slowly—everything must be carefully considered and in detail. However, leadership style is the one variable that an organization can change quickly. Fortunately, this change can make a significant difference, almost overnight.

Think about the best job you ever had and think about the person to whom you reported. Chances are if you liked the job, you liked your up-line. Now think about the worst job you ever had. Did you like your boss? Probably not. While CDOs can help manage change for an entire organization, they also manage groups of people that help them manage change for that entire organization. Treating people well helps you carry out more than what you can do by yourself within the organization. Do not forget this. Given all the effort spent to get resources and have people report to you, make *sure* you find ways to motivate and keep them!

Some people believe it is better to control employees and get the job done through direct means. That might work in a small team environment. But, when it comes to managing across the enterprise, you must lead differently. As we said earlier, this stuff is not easy. When you allow people to contribute and bring their ideas to the table, you open the floor to new alternatives.

Challenges to data governance

Both approaches present challenges. The top-down approach is often an overly bureaucratic and restrictive processes that imposes more work on staff members without necessarily proving tangible value. The mechanized bottom-up approach produces data summaries, but data professionals must invest the effort to analyze these summaries to isolate and document the discovered standards and rules.

Furthermore, some data governance programs set up processes and procedures that overwhelm an organization, which has the impractical effect of undermining the program's long-term effectiveness. Moreover, managers specify tactical milestones that reflect program implementation but struggle to define program targets tied to specific business requirements and measurable business goals and aims.

Most organizations have made considerable investments in IT, but few have yet made a strong commitment to information as a corporate resource. Because of the growth in computing power and the benefits it offers, most organizations have overlooked nurturing the support that computers sustain—information. It is as essential as the human, financial, and physical assets of the industrial age (Evernden and Evernden, 2012). Consequently, it is critical to conduct data governance in concert with other forms of governance.

A sound data strategy requires that the data contained in an organization's single source of truth (SSOT) is of high quality, granular, and standardized, and that multiple versions of the truth (MVOTs) are carefully controlled and derived from the same SSOT. Being able to set up an SSOT necessitates good governance for both data and technology. In the absence of proper management, some common problems arise:

- **Data definitions may be ambiguous and mutable.** With no concrete definition at the outset of what constitutes "truth," whether SSOT or MVOTs, stakeholders squander time and resources as they try to manage non-standard data.

- **Data rules are vague or inconsistently applied.** If rules for aggregating, integrating, and transforming data are unclear, misunderstood, or just ignored — mainly when data transformation involves multiple poorly defined steps — it is difficult to replicate changes and leverage information across the organization reliably.

- **Feedback loops for improving data transformation are absent.** Diverse groups can perform complex data analyses such as predictive modeling, and other groups can use the study for their work. Without mechanisms for making these outputs available to others — by, for example, integrating them into proper MVOTs — stakeholders may needlessly duplicate work or miss opportunities.

Who makes the call?

The CDO operates in large part by an organization's recognition that data is critical to business success. When an organization realizes it needs a CDO, the question of authority comes to the forefront almost at once. While many agree CDOs manage "all things data," there is still disagreement as to what responsibilities and decision rights the CDO has. Today, organizations struggle with describing their CDOs, with many falling back to traditional interpretations that include limiting CDOs to just data strategy, governance, and quality. However, unresolved issues are simmering with equity issues unaddressed, unresolved, and fraught with bureaucratic tension.

"Who are you to tell me what I can do with my data?" is something that many CDOs hear when they assume their new role. Their arrival sometimes triggers behaviors that range from passive resistance to outright conflict. Reminiscent of the early CIO days, CDOs face similar forces. While CIOs fought to set up authority over IT assets, CDOs fight to set up jurisdiction over data assets. For CIOs, this struggle lasted for quite some time, but today, virtually every organization understands that it must have a CIO and that the CIO sets the enterprise IT direction. However, CDOs are still new to the C-suite. They are only beginning to appear in organizations, and their roles, responsibilities, and authority vary. It is crucial when organizations start to set up a data management program that they name a data authority as one of the first and most critical first steps. Without giving CDOs the organizational power to make binding decisions about data, CDOs must fight skirmish after skirmish while never addressing enterprise problems.

To remove any ambiguity concerning a CDO's authority, organizations must set up and promote an explicit charter that defines a CDO's authorities, responsibilities, and accountabilities for all stakeholders. The charter sets up and defines the parameters for other working relationships across the C-suite and enterprise.

There is a valuable hierarchy associated with business-oriented data policies that describe and define how an organization manages its data assets—from giddy-up to whoa! Collectively, such artifacts define all phases of the data lifecycle: from requirements assessment and data acquisition planning to modeling to processing to storage and to final records disposition. Most importantly, however, is the idea that organizations should define data governance along strictly hierarchical lines and memorialize those reporting relationships in programmatic documentation:

- **Law.** A rule usually made by a government that is used to order how a society behaves.

- **Charter.** Delegated authority that describes the duties and powers that an entity (such as an organization or role) is authorized to lead.

- **Policy.** A set of officially approved ideas or plans.

- **Procedures.** A set of actions that is the official or accepted way of doing something.

- **Standards.** An established norm for technical systems that shows uniform technical criteria, methods, processes, and practices.

LAW

A rule, usually made by government, that is used to order the way in which a society behaves.

CHARTER

A detailed description of the duties and powers to be carried out by the person to whom authority is delegated

POLICY

A set of ideas or a plan of what to do in particular situations that has been officially ratified.

PROCEDURE

A Set of actions that is the official or accepted way of doing something

STANDARD

Is an established norm for technical systems that establishes uniform technical criteria, methods, processes and practices.

Figure 10. Delegated authorities

Determining decision rights and responsibilities are foundational for projects or programs. Stakeholders must know who can make decisions when they reach an impasse or decision point. Decision-making rules are often recorded in policies, which describe stakeholders, and assigning and enforcing related policies is equally important. Data management programs are no different. Having experience in this area for one type of project will enable you to extend it to other systems, both old and new, within your enterprise. As a best practice, it is essential that these projects are linked and that governance methods are consistent across the full range of information types, irrespective of the system of origin or where the data ends up.

Another best practice is the introduction of data stewardship, assigning specific responsibility and accountability to individuals who manage and generate revenue, improving service, and decreasing time to market. Organizations can often realize these benefits when they implement master data management (MDM) and enterprise content management (ECM) data quality and e-discovery projects. Any proactive data governance program must begin with an effort to value information as an asset.

To gain maximum leverage and value from customer data that is the subject of an MDM project, one must also consider how the organization intends to use that data as well as the legalities of doing so.

Deconflict the roles

Organizational structures change in response to an evolving environment. With each change, organizational models become increasingly more complicated. Eventually, unnecessarily complex organizational structures become unwieldy. Communication becomes difficult, and cooperation suffers (Boston Consulting Group, 2011). After some time, leaders realize people must cross organizational boundaries and work with one another. However, those same leaders have few solutions to the problem. Employees are left to figure things out on their own. Learning to work with people takes time, resources, and trust. And for most, resources are tight.

As tools to help people work with one another, organizational charters can help to clarify roles, responsibilities, and authorities. Such charters help everyone understand how people interact and who owns a decision. Organizational charters also help people have tough conversations and reduce organizational tension. They also clarify accountabilities and decision rights compared to data management. For example, an organizational charter informs everyone as to who can release data to the public. The charter names those who chair a data governance body and what their decision rights are. The charter sets up behavioral norms, expectations, and metrics to help everyone succeed. For example, an organizational charter would delineate the CDO and CIO roles.

Across our careers, we've seen many organizations forgo developing charters. And when people skip this step, problems almost always occur. These types of problems typically generate distrust and only hurt the work. So, we recommend that CDOs take the time to develop charters at the onset of their tenure. It will help them develop strong and lasting work relationships.

Measuring progress

Governing data management describes a top-down approach to designing, planning, populating, and managing the organization's approved data management metadata repository to describe the organization's data assets fully. These governance process areas foster data sharing, ensure compliant use of data, improve responsiveness to changes, and reduce data-related risks.

The organization must institute a robust and effective compliance program as evaluated through KPIs across the data lifecycle. Characteristics of effective data governance management are oversight, assurance of stakeholder collaboration, and facilitation of decision making for critical data subject areas. Primary data governance points of focus include the creation of new capabilities, processes for collaboration, evaluation, decision making, and the exercise of positive control over data assets. Data changes must be planned and controlled across the data lifecycle. The data lifecycle is quantitatively managed using KPIs for successful data management, and change impact analyses are regularly conducted.

Organizations suffer from data governance problems such as excessive compartmentalization, which leads to narrowly focused governance and parochial definitions that only represent a selected organizational population. Today, these problems are just getting worse with the advent of big data, cloud deployment models, mobility, and social data (Buytendijk, 2015).

Anytime data crosses an organizational boundary, CDOs must make sure that they control that data, whether sharing data among business units internally or publishing data to customers, partners, auditors, and regulatory bodies externally (Russom, 2008). Furthermore, we now live in the "age of accountability," which demands stricter oversight of data usage, an understanding of data lineage, quality, privacy, and security. Organizations are under renewed pressure to ensure the satisfaction of compliance and accountability requirements as the scope of data integration broadens. In response to this situation, many organizations are turning to data governance, which sets up policies and procedures for sharing data, as well as improving data quality, structure, and auditability.

Furthermore, the goal of some data governance programs is to enable an organization to treat data as an organizational asset. Achieving this goal demands many interim goals, most involving dramatic change. For example, data governance transforms an organization's data, its data management technology, data ownership, and the way the organization uses data. Sweeping changes and business transformations like these require a central organizational structure such as a data governance committee or board staffed with both business and technology people. The board must institute and enforce policies and procedures for the management and business use of data. And data governance is best coordinated together with IT governance and corporate governance. Becoming data-driven also requires strong organizational change management as it can be a completely different form of control.

Key takeaways

- **Make data the cornerstone.** It sounds simple, but it is not. This is the start of data-centric thinking. Put data first!

- **If data is valuable, treat it like it is valuable.** If you care about something, you keep track of it. You take care of it and you manage it.

- **Get data on the balance sheet.** Monetize your data. Get it on the balance sheet and make people understand that it adds or detracts from the bottom line.

- **Focus on the things that really hurt.** Do not become overwhelmed by everything that needs fixing. Focus on the things you can positively affect.

- **Know your people.** The trust you build with stakeholders will be worth every second you invest in them. They will make or break you.

- **Know what you have.** You cannot manage data if you do not know what you have. It is just that simple.

CHAPTER 9

Setting up Shop

"You can have data without information, but you cannot have information without data."

— Daniel Keys Moran, Science Fiction Writer

Organizations should rethink what they are doing and make some key changes. For example, organizations should recognize data management as a business function instead of an IT function. The organization needs to charge the CDO with developing the organization's data strategy and ensuring that this plan directly supports the organization's strategic goals and aims. As part of this change, data management requires executive leadership that reports to the organization's most senior leader, such as the CEO, as well as other C-level officers. Organizations should recruit a qualified CDO who reports within the C-suite at the same level as other resource managers: HR, Finance, IT, and the like.

Now more than ever, the ability to manage torrents of data is critical to an organization's success. But even with the emergence of data management functions and CDOs, most organizations are still behind the curve. Cross-industry studies show that, on average, less than half of all organizations use structured data to make decisions—and less than 1% of its unstructured data is analyzed or used at all. More than 70% of employees have access to information they should not, and analysts spend 80% of their time searching for and preparing data (DalleMule et al., 2017). Data breaches are common, rogue data sets propagate in silos, and organizations' data technology often misses the mark.

Let's get started

The idea of a plan seems easy enough. We caution CDOs, however, to follow the guidance that General Dwight D. Eisenhower offered, "In preparing for battle I have always found that plans are useless, but planning is indispensable" (Eisenhower, 1950). So, we encourage CDOs to concentrate on creating an organization that knows how to manage data across the lifecycle.

Plans are still important, but CDOs must avoid becoming fascinated by them and spending all their time producing a document. Remember, great plans that never get implemented are pipedreams, and organizations rarely have the patience for fantasies.

Where does it hurt?

Instead of spending significant resources on producing a strategy (document), we recommend CDOs review Goldratt's Theory of Constraints (TOC) and use it across their organizations. According to Goldratt, there is always at least one constraint in a system that needs attention and improvement. Organizations are, therefore, vulnerable because the weakest part can damage or break the whole organization. From this idea comes the popular idiom, "a chain is no stronger than its weakest link." Using the TOC will help CDOs find problematic areas and give CDOs options for getting some short-term wins. A practical tool for naming and measuring weak links is the DMM. CDOs can use the DMM to show weak areas, adjust, and repeat. If CDOs use the DMM over and over, their organizational score will improve over time.

Some practical issues

Organizational alignment is essential for CDOs. CDOs must do everything they can to ensure they are aligned with the business. *Nothing guarantees mission failure more than aligning the CDO to the wrong part of the organization.* No CDO wants to be put into a position of failure, but this happens far too often. When the alignment is wrong, the entire data organization runs at suboptimal levels and can suffocate or outright kill an organization's data effort.

Conversely, when the CDO is aligned to the business, employees invest more of their personal time, talents, and energy into meeting or exceeding organizational goals.

New CDOs have a million things to manage, and they can be overwhelming. There are, though, some practical things that CDOs must do. We recommend that CDOs address the following issues as soon as they can:

- Securing executive approval
- Writing an executive order
- Passing legislation
- Establishing CDO authority
- Deconflicting roles

Securing executive approval

On a practical level, how does one charter a CDO? There are at least two several ways: one is to have a chief executive issue a mandate, and the other is to have a legislative body set up rules. Both methods work for private and public sectors even though each sector may call the methods different things.

For example, in the private sector, a CEO may make an executive decision and set up a CDO by edict. Alternatively, a board of directors may order the CEO to create the CDO. Similar methods exist in the public sector. For example, a president, governor, or mayor may issue an executive order and set up a CDO. Alternatively, a legislative body may pass a law creating a CDO.

Executive mandate

In place of lawmaking abilities, chief executives historically have used executive orders to promote policy agendas. As with proclamations and memoranda, executive orders are the chief executive's primary tools for the management and mobilization of organizational resources. In the US, an executive order is a directive issued by a chief executive, typically the US President or a state governor, without requiring legislative approval. A mayor of a city could also issue an executive order. An executive order instructs the government how to work within the parameters of the relevant charter or constitution. In the private sector, the chief executive can issue similar instructions through corporate policy.

In this way, organizations can charter CDOs by executive mandate. Remember, however, CDOs must be sure they are clear what kind of outcome they want. For example, executive mandates are something other executives can overturn. In other words, they could be temporary, or worse, short-lived. Chief executives can change their minds and reverse, repeal, or otherwise change their instructions. It is an easy thing to do because there is only one decision-maker, and the person can change their mind.

Also, another chief executive could undo a decision that predecessor made. So, CDOs should look for long-term solutions to their authority and not rely exclusively on what the boss says. The boss will likely move on, and then what happens to the CDO under a new regime? Enough said.

Set up rules

The other way to charter the CDO is through a legislative process. A good example of this is the US Congress. Congress has lawmaking authority granted to it by the US Constitution. Laws serve many purposes and functions in society, including setting up standards, keeping order, resolving disputes, and protecting liberties and rights. Public sector CDOs can work with their legislatures to create laws that establish CDOs and their authorities. For example, the federal government created the Open Government Data Act, which directs the government to appoint a CDO for each federal agency. The law also describes the powers federal CDOs have.

There are legislative bodies in the private sector as well. Corporate boards serve as rulemaking bodies for companies. While the rules vary company-to-company, boards set rules or policies that companies must follow. Private sector CDOs could work with their corporate boards to define private sector CDOs.

Who reports to whom?

Until recently, many saw the CDO as a technical role, and it is quite common to see CDOs reporting directly to CIOs. However, organizations now align their CDOs closer to business and farther from technology. For example, a few organizations, like the Commonwealth of Virginia, position their CDO and CIO alongside one another. They are peered roles. Both report to an executive responsible for operational components of the state. This alignment has some advantages. For example, the CDO can focus on data issues and the CIO can focus on technology issues. Second, this alignment allows for greater accountability. Organizations following this alignment can better distinguish investments in technology *versus* data management. This alignment is a convenient way to ensure checks and balances between the organizations.

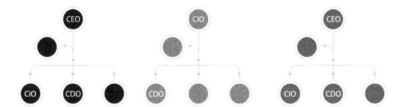

Figure 11. CDO alignment

A less common alignment is when the CIO reports to the CDO. We are not aware of any organization following this model, but this orientation is intriguing. First, this alignment would ensure the business still is in control of its data and decision-making. Second, this alignment better supports the assertion that *data is the business*. Technology is a *tool* and an enabler.

Make a plan

Having a CDO and a data management function is a start, but if the organization wants to be fully effective, the organization needs a coherent strategy for organizing, governing, analyzing, and deploying an organization's information assets. A data strategy typically includes a vision statement, goals, aims, priorities, scope, defined business benefits, a data management framework, high-level roles, responsibilities, and governance needs (Aiken & Harbour, 2017). It often includes a description of the approach used to develop the data management program, the high-level compliance approach, and a high-level sequence plan (roadmap). A data strategy usually encompasses, at a minimum, these aspects:

- **Version.** Whole number changes reflect iterations with iteration improvements and clarifications to the right of the iteration cycle number—that is, 4.3 stands for the third version of the fourth iteration.

- **Vision.** Vision is concerned with what the organization aspires to be. Its purpose is to set out a view of the future to enthuse, gain commitment from, and improve the performances of its workers (Johnson, 2011).

- **Mission.** A mission provides employees and stakeholders with clarity about the overall purpose and *raison d'être* of the organization (Johnson, 2011).

- **Goals.** Goals are open-ended statements of what one wishes to do with no quantification of what is to be achieved and no timeframe for completion (Hill, 2011).

- **Objectives.** Objectives are the end results of planned activity. They say what is to be carried out and by when, and they should be quantified if possible (Hill, 2011).

- **Plan.** A plan is a statement that prescribes specific actions to be taken to implement established policies (Project Management Institute, 2016).

- **Priorities.** Facts or conditions that are given or merit attention before competing alternatives make up priorities (Merriam Webster, 2016).

- **Scope.** The scope is the sum of the products, services, and results to be reached as a project. (See also "project scope" and "product scope") (Project Management Institute, 2013).

Data strategy needs to reinforce the use of standards and outline the overall governance framework the organization will employ to make decisions about implementation. It should also consider initial implementation considerations, such as architectural initiatives and technology transformation initiatives that are underway or planned, and it needs to define a sequence plan to guide implementation.

The organization's data strategy must evolve as the needs of the organization change. As a result, organizations will be able to affect change through close collaboration of different organizational components. Cooperation is essential to building and keeping an effective data management program. One example of improved collaboration is broader, executive-led responsibility for data quality reflected throughout the data lifecycle.

The most useful data management strategies are those that are visibly and actively endorsed by executive management and supported by mandatory organizational policy. In effect, these strategies are institutionalized. The ensuing collaborative project—developing the data management strategy—is a powerful mechanism for clarifying executive decisions and directives, as well as fast-tracking the data management program. In the ideal instance, all key players have had a voice in the process. They reach agreement on goals, priorities, and measures. They secure administrative approval for capabilities that need improving, and all relevant stakeholders understand the impacts of the plan.

Get some top cover

No matter where you work, you report to someone. You may report to more than one boss. CDOs are no different. They have bosses too. And like everyone, whether they think their boss is brilliant or a bore, CDOs must manage those relationships, especially if CDOs intend to start an enterprise data effort. As we have discussed, changing culture is a very tricky business, and there are equities at stake. So, CDOs must get all the help they can from every quarter, including their bosses.

In simple terms, CDOs must get bureaucratic protection and sponsorship from an organizational champion. The higher the leadership support, the better. Having executive top cover like this will help CDOs weather organizational storms and navigate bureaucratic minefields. Having top cover also helps CDOs gain and sustain organizational inertia and secure the buy-in for change. Be wary, though. No matter how good CDOs believe their ideas are, others in the organization must believe in them too.

According to Ajit Kambil (2018), there are specific kinds of sponsorship that CDOs should consider: innovation, collaboration, leadership development, and branding. Each type of support aligns with the four sides of the CDO as a strategist, change agent, steward, and operator. In this model, patronage lies at the intersection of the four aspects of CDO leadership:

- **Reputation.** The moment you walk in the door, your reputation follows you. As the saying goes, you only get one chance to make a first impression. Some of the people you meet become acquaintances, and some become friends. But everyone has an opinion about you — and it goes as far back as your childhood days. Your reputation tells others how well do you play in the sandbox? Before you can even make a case for your strategy, people must believe you can work with others to get things done. Once you get buy-in for your plan, reputation pivots and becomes all about how well you deliver on what you promise — in big and small ways. A little project for a big sponsor can take you farther than a huge project with just your team involved. Stand and deliver, and your reputation will follow.

- **Innovation.** Innovation brings to life something new that enables an organization to move from the present to a new and different future. There can be many types of innovation that create many different futures. When sponsoring change, it is essential to choose a locus of innovation that is aligned with the strategy and goals of the company. For example, if an organization focuses its approach on improving productivity, processes, and supply chain efficiencies, network innovations are likely to deliver the desired results. If the strategic focus of the company is on growing market share, then channel and customer experience innovations may be more aligned to the strategy.

- **Collaboration.** Sponsoring collaboration and connection within or across organizations can enable critical access to ideas and other resources that help companies innovate or improve the execution of initiatives. For example, many exciting opportunities now lie outside the boundaries of traditional functions and organizations and at the intersection of different fields. In academia, provosts and deans regularly encourage collaborations across different colleges and departments to meet changing demands for new knowledge, and research CDOs should do the same. Create collaboration across organization silos that might not only enable innovation but also reduce inefficiencies in the organization resulting from disparate systems and processes.

- **Leadership.** The term is self-explanatory: a leader must lead. In the context of sponsorship, though, a leader must lead not only the team but anyone else needed to get the job done, even when those folks do not report to them. Leadership in the sponsorship context must include getting buy-in for your ideas and strategies that will set the stage for organizational change.

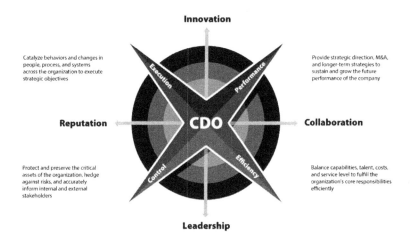

Innovation

Catalyze behaviors and changes in people, process, and systems across the organization to execute strategic objectives

Provide strategic direction, M&A, and longer-term strategies to sustain and grow the future performance of the company

Reputation — **CDO** — **Collaboration**

Execution

Performance

Control

Efficiency

Protect and preserve the critical assets of the organization, hedge against risks, and accurately inform internal and external stakeholders

Balance capabilities, talent, costs, and service level to fulfil the organization's core responsibilities efficiently

Leadership

Figure 12. Sponsorship

These four pillars are the directional levers of the CDO—think of a compass. They let you know at any given time where you stand in the grand scheme of the sponsorship world. Based on where you want to go, the needle direction shows which of the four skills needs focus. Those skills are execution, performance, control, and efficiency. While the illustration presents these skills as immutable, we suggest that they should shift so, just as with a compass.

For instance, control rests between reputation and leadership, and efficiency sits between leadership and collaboration. However, sometimes it is better to allow people whom you are leading to implement ideas creatively; you often get better work out of them by taking the initiative. Having more creative solutions can make for a better reputation. Likewise, planned collaboration can be useful—for instance, when you schedule a project planning or brainstorming session. Encouraging collaboration can lead people to speak more regularly with each other and "dream" without a specific project or plan on the table. While collaboration can be a solution finder, it also can be an issue spotter. Once you know what issues there are, you can work together to solve them, which of course, means more collaboration.

The four 'directions'—execution, performance, control, and efficiency—exist for more than just periodic updates. You should use and gather inputs regularly throughout the change process. As a CDO, draw on these tools when you must adjust—they are yours to command! Use them and be prepared to combine these tools when it works to your advantage.

Show them how to do it

Because data is something poorly understood by many people, there is often a lack of qualified leadership to make decisions about data. The lack of qualified decision-makers perpetuates itself in large part because there are few educational programs at colleges and universities addressing data management. Lacking foundational education leads to a conundrum: without requisite data KSAs for position candidates, how will organizations know whom to hire to help them up their data smarts? Lacking foundational KSAs impedes organizational decision making across the organization and engenders negative results.

No matter where you work, you report to someone— maybe even to two or three bosses. Whether you think your boss is brilliant or a bore, the fact is that you must manage the relationship with your boss if you want to advance your career.

Realize that you are more dependent on your boss than your boss is on you, because your boss holds the key to your short-term future. Not only can your boss release you at any time—especially in today's economy—but your boss can also unconsciously ostracize you by not keeping you in the communication loop and by giving all the desirable projects to others. When your boss senses that communication between the two of you is not going well and situations have not been resolved, you may notice them going to your colleagues instead.

Therefore, manage the relationship with your boss; otherwise, you will not last long in your position. In a large company, you might be able to transfer to a different position with a different boss; but then you will just manage another boss, and you could end up repeating the cycle.

Key takeaways

- **Try something different**. Organizational change is immensely hard, and if you keep doing the same thing over and over, you can expect to get the same results.

- **Figure out where you are**. Perform a data assessment to learn where your organization is on the data maturity scale. No one must boil the ocean. Determine where the biggest pains are and address them first.

- **Establish your authorities**. When you charter the office, make sure that your authorities are clearly defined and there is no equivocation.

- **Get an executive sponsor**. This is a must! Without it, you may have a painful and rather short-lived experience.

- **Communicate.** Tell stories that get others to share their ideas and problems. Talk and listen. Then do it again with a different group of people.

- **Get out of your office**. Meet with people at their locations and their convenience.

- **See what sticks!** Develop an entrepreneurial approach and a mindset of "Let's try it." Just like that old saying suggests, "Throw spaghetti against the wall and, if it sticks, it is done." Try new things, fail quickly, and pivot to something else. Experimentation with different approaches helps to keep your program new and improved.

CHAPTER 10

What the *Bleep* Just Happened?

"We're entering a new world in which data may be more important than software."

— Tim O'Reilly, Founder, O'Reilly Media

Data management is not a glamorous or sexy discipline. What is? Data analytics. Any data management professional who has ever tried to compete with visualization or analytic capabilities understands this. Impassioned data leaders often have the wind sucked from their sails when colorful visuals leap from the screen and prime the imaginations of every executive in the room. Often, analytics tools win the day—and the money. Only recently are there enough data professionals in leadership positions to push back and ask tough questions about the underlying data and how it affects the calculus. So, in this chapter, we will look at the role of the CDO and data analytics, how the two coexist, and how CDOs can use their work to lay a solid data foundation and prepare the organization for business analytics.

As organizations mature in their data practices, they encounter fewer 'fires' and typically have more opportunity to delve into problem causation. Here, analytics becomes a valuable tool for digging into the root causes of problems. Rather than stopping at just identifying the issue and addressing a symptom, root cause analysis allows the organization to better understand the problem and how best to fix it. This method also enables the prevention of issues further down the analytics pipeline.

Using analytics to understand the source of problems is the perfect place for organizations to apply advanced technical solutions. Enabling analytics at this level has the added benefit of potentially solving problems that may not yet have even arisen, saving more time and money—and profane language. Understanding the real problem is where many organizations often get stuck.

An answer for every question

The four types of data analytics can support different decision scenarios:

- **Descriptive:** Answers basic questions about "what happened" in a project or set of programs.

- **Diagnostic:** Answers the question related to "why" something happened by comparing historical data from one program against the data of other programs.

- **Prescriptive:** Begins to flesh out what actions to take by looking at data, sometimes from outside the organization, as a means of guiding the organization toward some strategic direction.

- **Predictive:** Describes what is likely to happen based on a course of action and data, either internal from earlier programs or external from similar companies and programs.

Follow the Yellow Brick Road

People depict data lifecycles as unidirectional or sometimes bi-directional. Organizations create it, change it, support it, store it, and remove it. And once they remove it, what else could happen? The same could be said of a few other steps of that lifecycle. It turns out that data could do quite a lot more. As projects and systems are created and acted on, data has tendrils to tell us a lot about what is happening; it can reflect how in-depth the system is being used, whether things are working correctly, and how people are using it. And for all those pieces of information, we can then reflect on how close the answers match our first assumptions, our changes in assumption, and our continued use of that system.

Success in technology often is only viewed at the time of implementation, and after the first bug fixes are complete, but long-term success, usage, and system consumption are more critical. When eyes are no longer watching closely, problems can erupt quickly and painfully with expensive results.

If we only look at our current systems, then we are looking at snapshots taken in hindsight. These measures can't tell us how we are doing now and how we can do in the future—or can they? Most organizations use data to reflect on how they are doing, which is essential. People can use data to reflect on the past as well. Sometimes the oldest concepts are the easiest to revive, renew, and relaunch. Those distinct possibilities are missed as well when current snapshots are the only items reviewed.

To be clear, this is not about data analytics. Understanding the information in our systems can tell us about both what has happened or what is currently happening. This is about data strategy. It's not enough to reflect on the current snapshot. Instead, we suggest an approach that reaches back to past performance, programs, and systems as well as future potential. The full spectrum of an organization's prowess and possibility can be measured, contemplated, and acted on, all with the help of data.

Data analytics—it adds up

Data analytics is a loaded phrase. People use the phrase all the time, believing that data analytics are presentations that show lines, colors, numbers, etc. Pictures are not analytics. They are representations of information, presentations of calculations, and counts of things. If you mix the pictures together before you present the information, you first must understand what you are trying to show. Otherwise, how can you know what the picture should look like? An analytic is a form of scientific inquiry with a formal process for design.

Step 1: Define your question

Data analytics starts with a question. The question posed should be measurable, precise, and succinct. It should qualify or disqualify potential solutions to the stated problem. Consider this business case: A company's program costs continue to rise. The company offers proposals that exceed the customer's ability to pay for the company's services. A defining question might be: How can the company reduce its costs to meet the customer's budget?

But data analytics applies to many other domains:

- How did life begin?
- What makes us human?

- How do we get more energy from the sun?
- What is at the bottom of a black hole?
- Is time travel possible?

Step 2: Establish measurement priorities

This step has two crucial components: the choice of what to measure and determining how to measure it. Let's look at each in more depth.

Selecting what to measure

Using the contractor example, think about what data is needed to answer the question. In this example, you must know what costs could be adjusted to reduce the overall cost. For example, labor costs, overhead costs, and profit are a few. When you decide what to cut, you might also consider changes to reduce costs. For example, if you swap personnel on a project, would the customer object?

Determining how to measure it

Thinking about how you measure your data is just as important as deciding what to measure, especially before the data collection phase, because your measuring process either backs up or discredits your analysis later. Key questions to ask for this step include:

- How long is the period of analysis?
- What is your unit of measure?
- What factors should you include?

Step 3: Collect data

Now you need data. As you collect and organize data, keep these points in mind:

- Before you collect new data, make sure to check whether you already have access.

- Set data storage, naming, and other conventions.

- Follow existing protocols if you must collect more data.

- Design a template for collecting observations.

- Organize your data with other metadata, such as dates, locations, and notes. This will help you interpret the data later.

Step 4: Analyze data

After you collect the needed data, you must be sure that the data is in a consistent format. If it is not, you must normalize your data with several processing techniques. Preserve the meaning of your data as you transform it into new formats. Look for correlations and use statistical calculations to understand their meanings. As you manipulate your data, you will learn more about its meaning. So, prepare to change your original question. Focus on better ways to answer your question using trends, correlations, variations, and outliers. This step depends on the software you use.

Step 5: Interpret results

After you have analyzed your data, you must interpret the results. Remember that analysis is not absolute. Data analysis uses statistical probability, and all you can do is reject a hypothesis. There is always a chance that your hypothesis may not be true. Ask these questions:

- Did your data answer your question?
- How did the data answer the question?
- What constraints are there on your conclusions?

When you have answers to your questions, you can use the information to inform your decisions. You can use this process to quantify, qualify, and improve your decisions.

Warning: dashboards may blind you!

Many organizations see dashboards and become blinded by their dizzying array of graphs, numbers, and pizazz. Only later do they realize that all the pretty lights were distracting them from the genuine issues. If you start to measure the organization's work, be sure to start slowly. Measure the things that truly matter to the organization, do not measure everything just because you can.

Technology also limits itself by trapping data in the same systems that captured it. While technology is essential, executives overlook or underestimate the value of data management. Without such appreciation, data initiatives falter and do not deliver.

Here is a simple and all too common story. Department of Transportation data associated with designing safer roads is left unused because accident reports prepared by law enforcement officials were not made accessible in a usable form. Moreover, neither the highway department nor the law enforcement organization had the budget or the legislative authority to develop standards to improve the data.

Key takeaways

- **Dig deep**. Look for root causes to your data problems and spend less time solving superficial problems.

- **Focus on the data**. Before analyzing your data, make sure it is ready for analysis. Making decisions on bad data leads to bad outcomes.

- **Know your questions**. Tools do not read minds, so know the questions you want answered before spending resources on analytic tools and efforts.

CHAPTER 11

Federal Changes

"It is a capital mistake to theorize before one has data."

— Sherlock Holmes

We originally developed this section for the International Society of Chief Data Officers. Our convictions about FEPA impact on government, the public, and society remain unchanged, and we hope you find the material reproduced here helpful.

While many Americans were shoveling their driveways and sidewalks from a series of winter storms, the federal government closed, the President signed the Foundations for Evidence-Based Policymaking Act of 2018 (FEPA). Much of what we know about the new law and its impact is still to be seen, but several things are readily clear. First, the role of the CDO is now incorporated into federal law and separated from the role of the CIO. Second, government data is now open by default, and the federal government must keep its data in open standards-based formats. Third, the law requires setting up data management rigor in governmental "evidence-based decision-making." Fourth, the Act fully recognizes the value and use of data in agency operations. Finally, the law expects that, collectively, these efforts will improve governmental decision making and overall effectiveness.

FEPA's broad requirements present federal agencies with new opportunities and challenges. On the one hand, some enthusiastically support the arrival of CDOs and their assignment over national data. On the other hand, some are concerned that without new funding, the federal government could not respond to these new expectations. There is little doubt that these changes will affect digital data across agency data systems as well as data in physical formats. Compliance with FEPA requirements could require levels of effort reaching those spent for Y2K compliance in the late nineties.

Foundations for Evidence-Based Policy Act of 2018 (FEPA)

This section is a synopsis of the new legislation, the authors' views of the new law, and a preliminary assessment of the law and the impacts it may have on government, industry, and the public. We summarize the legislation's noteworthy features, examine how the new law differs from earlier legislation, and review the requirement to expand the use of data across the federal landscape. Then we show outstanding questions we believe deserve further analysis and clarification.

It exclusively reflects the authors' thoughts and opinions. We received help in the form of review comments from many colleagues, and we especially thank the Bipartisan Policy Center's Dr. Nick Hart. He was one of the legislation's strongest proponents.

Let's begin with a clarifying note instigated by one of our reviewers. Natalie Evans Harris, former Senior Policy Advisor in the presidential Office of Science and Technology Policy, and now BrightHive's COO—noted that we should explicitly differentiate between open data laws and federal data laws. Open data is a subset of the suite of federal data laws. FEPA is a federal data law and is more comprehensive than open data laws. This important distinction is obscured by the new law's use of the acronym OPEN (Open, Public, Electronic, and Necessary). Evidence-based policymaking addresses processes far beyond open data. It is about data's use as a strategic asset.

There are only a handful of federal data laws requiring the government to share data with its constituents. The first significant law was the Freedom of Information Act (FOIA) in 1967. FOIA requires federal agencies to show requested information to the requestor unless it falls under one of nine exemption categories (5 U.S. Code § 552). Years later, the federal government passed the Federal Funding

Accountability and Transparency Act of 2006 (FFATA) to empower every American with the ability to hold the government accountable for each spending decision. This law resulted in the data-sharing site, USASpending.gov, where the public can use government-provided tools to analyze more than 80% of annual government spending. The list of laws also includes GPRA (1993) and CIPSEA (2002).

A more recent data law was the Digital Accountability and Transparency Act of 2014 (The DATA Act). The DATA Act requires the federal government to transform and report its spending information into open data. The DATA Act also amended the Federal Funding Accountability and Transparency Act of 2006, addressing two fundamental issues:

1. The Act required the Treasury Department (TRE) and the White House Office of Management and Budget (OMB) to set up government-wide data standards for reporting expenditures to TRE, OMB, and the General Services Administration (GSA). When the government collects data from the public, TRE and OMB publish that information at no cost to the public via the internet.

2. The Act tried to standardize data that contractors and grantees report to the federal government. The law required OMB to determine whether data standards might relieve compliance costs for

financial reporting. OMB concluded that rules were critical and would help control costs.

The DATA Act uncovered the need for standardization but did not address the lack of universal data standards. Instead, the government continued to employ ad hoc, agency-specific policies, procedures, and markings to safeguard, mark, and control its data that introduced a confusing bureaucratic patchwork of inconsistent markings, incongruent processes to share data, and different standards to safeguard data.

In 2018, Congress passed the FEPA to address many of the gaps left by the DATA Act, and adds some new and potentially compelling elements to federal data implementation and use. FEPA follows a 2017 bipartisan commission report to Congress that advocated:

> *A future in which rigorous evidence is created efficiently, as a routine part of government operations, and used to construct effective public policy. Advances in technology and statistical methodology, coupled with a modern legal framework and a commitment to transparency, make it possible to do this while simultaneously providing stronger protections for the privacy and confidentiality of the people, businesses, and organizations from which the government collects information (American Statistical Association, 2017).*

The commission focused on improving how data is used to generate evidence in support of federal policies and programs. Additional support for FEPA arrived in the 2018 President's Management Agenda, which called for the development of a long-term national data strategy and for the government to leverage data as a strategic asset (Hart and Shaw, 2018). Though this legislation seemed slightly "out of the blue," according to a representative from the Data Coalition (The Data Coalition, n.d.), the group worked for more than three years with help from both political parties to help shape FEPA and position it for success in Congress. The Data Coalition is a group that advocates for the increased use of open standards by the federal government.

The following table is reproduced with permission from the Bipartisan Policy Center and summarizes the components of the commission's recommendations as described in FEPA.

Topic	Bill Section	CEP No.
Strengthening Privacy Protections		
Establishing an Agency Official for Data Policy	101(a) (§314)	3-3
Designation of Chief Data Officers	202(e) (§3520)	3-3
Codification of Statistical Policy Directive #1	302(a) (§3563 and §3572(b))	3-4
Conduct of Comprehensive Risk	303(a) (§3582)	3-1

Topic	Bill Section	CEP No.
Assessment and Analysis of Data Sensitivity		
Improving Secure Access to Data		
Establishing the Advisory Committee on Data for Evidence Building	101(a) (§315)	4-2
Creating and update Data Inventories with Metadata	202(d) (§3511)	4-5
Making Data Available for Statistical Activities	303(a) (§3581)	2-3
Developing a Single Process for Researcher Access to Data	303(a) (§3583)	2-8
Improving Transparency About Projects Using Confidential Data	303(a) (§3583(a)(6))	4-3
Enhancing Evidence-Building Capacity		
Requiring Agencies to Produce Evidence-Building Plans (learning agendas)	101(a) (§312)	5-2
Designation of Evaluation Officers and Requirements for Written Evaluation Policies	101(a) (§313)	5-1
Generation of an Inventory of Evidence-Building Units	101(c)	5-1
Establishing a Chief Data Officer Council	202(f) (§3 520A)	5-3
Improving Standard for Data Confidentiality and Disclosure Practices	302(a) (§3562)	5-3

TITLE I: Federal Evidence-Building Activities

The federal government engages in a wide variety of activities and, where possible, tries to measure its performance in quantitative terms. For example, the US Department of Commerce (DOC) conducts the Population and Housing Census every ten years to present a count of every person living in the US. Similarly, the Bureau of Justice Statistics sends a report describing justice systems, crime, criminal offenders, and victims of crime, and the Bureau of Transportation Statistics prepares a report describing airline on-time performance, pirates at sea, transportation safety and availability, and more. These reports and many others are used to measure the health and welfare of the US. They are critical inputs to legislative and executive decision making, specifically when it comes to building federal budgets and administering services across the country.

Collectively, the analysis behind these reports is known as *evidence-building activities*. These functions include the collection, compilation, processing, analysis, and dissemination of data to create general-purpose, policy- and program-specific statistics. Evidence-building activities also include program evaluation, research, policy- and program-related analysis, performance measurement, and public health surveillance. Federal evidence-building is highly decentralized, requiring each agency to carry out all the functions. While many departments and agencies have some ability to undertake at least some of this work, not every department and agency can perform them all to the consistently high, professional levels required by legislation.

Similarly, organizing principles vary by department and agency. For example, some departments have set up centralized offices for implementing one or more of these functions, while other departments have assigned evidence-building duties across program areas. Departments conduct most statistical activities across mission areas, such as health or energy, and the statistical methods that agencies use also vary by agency and department.

Then there are federal agencies considered to be Federal Statistical Agencies (FSA). Their activities are the collection, compilation, processing, or analysis of information for statistical purposes (Confidential Information Protection and Statistical Efficiency Act of 2002 (P.L. 107-347, Section 502(8)). Within these agencies, more than 120 analytical components are likely to be changed by the new legislation. The table below shows agencies likely to have the most disruption from the FEPA.

Agency	Federal Department
Census Bureau (Census)*	Commerce
Bureau of Economic Analysis (BEA)*	Commerce

Agency	Federal Department
Bureau of Labor Statistics (BLS)*	Labor
Bureau of Justice Statistics (BJS)	Justice
Bureau of Transportation Statistics (BTS)	Transportation
Economic Research Service (ERS)	Agriculture
Energy Information Administration (EIA)	Energy
National Agricultural Statistics Service (NASS)	Agriculture
National Center for Education Statistics (NCES)	Education
National Center for Health Statistics (NCHS)	Health and Human Services
National Center for Science and Engineering Statistics (NCSES)	National Science Foundation
Office of Research, Evaluation, and Statistics (ORES)	Social Security Administration
Statistics of Income Division (SOI)	Treasury

Note: An * denotes Designated Statistical Agencies (DSA) from federal statistical agencies.

Under Title I of FEPA, *all* federal agencies must manage their data using industry best practices, to analyze the data regularly, and to use the results to inform policymaking. These practices are intended to encourage using government data for measuring and understanding outcomes, rather than merely counting outputs and activities.

Federal agencies must develop plans around statistical questions and appoint officials who represent agency equities as they relate to analytical inquiries. Agencies must name data that they propose using to conduct qualified analyses. Researchers must also describe the methods they expect to use, legal obstacles that could impede their work, the plan they intend to follow, and any supporting information the Director of the OMB may ask.

Additionally, there is a requirement for a non-partisan chief evaluation officer who serves as a plan and implementation evaluator with proven domain ability. The selected individual is expected to correlate program evaluation activities to data production and data quality improvements over time. This positive structural enhancement is like the European Union's (EU) requirement for a neutral data quality official for all organizations.

Title I also requires OMB to establish an advisory council that reviews, analyzes, and makes recommendations for promoting the use of data for evidence-based decisions. The group is called the Advisory Committee on Data for Evidence Building (the Committee). Membership consists of thirteen participants with at least three federal CDOs.

The Committee also includes a single CIO to ensure continuity with IT.

TITLE II: Open Government Data Act

Open, Public, Electronic, and Necessary (OPEN) Government Data Act

Title II of FEPA is the OPEN Government Data Act. OPEN data is content that people can use without restriction. People can change and share OPEN data with anyone for any purpose. The federal government collects an enormous variety of data types to deliver services to its citizens. Many argue that the government has not used its data enough. With the passage of FEPA, federal data must be open and available, by default, for others to use, including other government agencies. OPEN data also includes access to analog data (i.e., not in digital form).

Where FOIA enables access to government data, by request in its original form, FEPA makes data electronically available. No specific application needed, regardless of its original type. Instead of using exempted data categories like those found in FOIA, the federal government must now develop a release process that ensures that the government does not release sensitive information as part of OPEN data.

FEPA's overall legislative intent includes increased transparency, self-empowerment, new or improved products and services, potential economic innovation, and new knowledge and growth areas. The Open Government Data Act is the part of FEPA that details how open data will work for federal data. For instance, Title II requires the government to supply three new foundational capabilities:

- A government-wide data inventory
- A new CDO role
- A data governance body that is known as the Chief Data Officer Council (CDO Council)

Data inventory and federal data catalog

All organizations keep inventory, especially for assets that are valuable. Organizations track information about their inventory, typically across the entire lifecycle of their processes. Inventory often includes an organization's physical assets like automobiles, buildings, and raw materials. Inventories also hold things used in daily activities, finished products, raw materials, or products for sale.

Data is now legislated to also be treated as an asset. Simply put, federal data has monetary value, and organizations must track data and its value. Data lets organizations know what they have. It also allows them to see what others need and provide it to them, either to save them money or to potentially charge them to use it. In these cases, data can be just as valuable, sometimes more, than physical products and the processes that produce them.

To that end, the Open Government Data Act requires agencies to keep an inventory of their data assets. Agencies must inventory and give their data holdings to a centralized federal data catalog that OMB administers. From there, other federal agencies, researchers, and the public can discover data that might be valuable. In this way, federal agencies can give better access to their data to everyone, including other agencies, and decrease the costs required to create the same data assets across several federal agencies.

Chief Data Officer

Data already supports strategic and operational efforts every day, from the largest and most prominent organizations like the Department of Defense (DoD) to the most obscure like the U.S. Board on Geographic Names (BGN). Data is also a key input for the creation and management of strategy and direction for organizations.

Effective use of data requires decision-makers have access to high quality, fit-for-purpose data. Well-formed data can include data from other agencies with different charters, authority, and compliance requirements. The complete view of business-relevant, high-quality data needs to be accessible by the right decision-makers to determine, update, and refine data-driven policy based upon measured results under changing environmental conditions. To that end, the new law requires every federal agency to name an individual who serves as the CDO. The CDO must:

- Set standards for data formats, negotiate terms for data sharing, and develop processes for data publishing;

- Coordinate with any agency officials responsible for using, protecting, disseminating, and generating data;

- Review the impact of agency IT infrastructure on data accessibility and coordinate with each agency's CIO to reduce barriers that inhibit data accessibility;

- Maximize the use of data in the agency to support evidence-based analysis, cybersecurity, and operational improvement;

- Get and support training and certification related to confidential information protection and statistical efficiency; and

- Handle overall data lifecycle management.

Chief Data Officer Council

Data governance is more than clarifying who 'stewards' data and associated decisions—instead, data governance works to optimize the value and use of data. By itself, data is the raw ingredient for improving business performance, and the responsibility for managing those resources falls on the business side.

While more organizations talk about data governance, those same organizations recognize that governance is technically complex, organizationally challenging, and politically sensitive. Compounding matters, getting executive support for data governance is critical, and unfortunately, executives don't often realize how important this business process is. Most often, data governance lands in IT hands by default. When organizations define data as a byproduct of information technology, data typically becomes an object of computing and is treated like other IT assets.

However, FEPA separates business problems and technical problems using the Council as a moderator. The Council requires that the government recognize data as the source material that enables and improves business processes, decisions, and interactions. Additionally, FEPA recognizes that data *must* remain a business asset where business takes the decisions concerning its acquisition, use, and disposition in the pursuit of generating the highest possible return on taxpayer investments.

The Council is composed of a chair appointed by the Director OMB, CDOs from each agency, two representatives for all federal CIOs and chief evaluation officers, and the Administrator of the Office of Electronic Government (OEG). The Council meets regularly and sets policy for:

- Establishing government-wide best practices for the use, protection, dissemination, and generation of data;

- Promoting and encouraging data sharing agreements between agencies;

- Showing ways agencies can improve the production of data for analysis and policymaking;

- Consulting with the public and engaging with private users of government data;

- Consulting other stakeholders on how to improve access to federal data; and

- Finding and evaluating new technological solutions for improving the collection and use of data.

Expanding the CDO role

Within the new legislation, there is a small and seemingly insignificant reference. Most people might glance over the citation, but it's worth a second look. Specifically, the law says the following:

(5) carry out the requirements of the agency under subsections (b) through (d), (f), and (i) of section 3506, section 3507, and section 3511;

These references describe the requirements for government efficiency, collection, and planning as they relate to federal data management. What this means is that FEPA formally requires CDOs to set the policies and procedures across the entire data lifecycle from planning a data collection through final records disposition.

In some cases, this means CDOs take a more active and direct role. For example, CDOs must communicate regularly with the public to ensure that an agency's data collection is necessary and not overly burdensome. CDOs, in cooperation with the agency Chief Financial Officer (CFO), are also required to develop "a full and accurate accounting of information technology expenditures" and goals for improving information resource management's contribution to the productivity, efficiency, and effectiveness of government operation.

TITLE III: Confidential Information Protection and the Statistical Efficiency Act of 2018

FEPA's scope is considerable and affects every part of the federal government; therefore, oversight and coordination are essential to its success. OMB oversees and coordinates the development of policies to help lead these efforts. OMB expects to develop, document, and make transparent business processes for all federal agencies to ensure all agencies support the same rules and implement consistent programs. FEPA also extends the notion of a statistical agency for all agencies to centralize their data. Additionally, agency heads will supply OMB reports as needed, while designated statistical agencies (DSA) will submit annual reports to OMB, the Committee on Oversight and Government Reform of the House of Representatives, and the Committee on Homeland Security and Governmental Affairs of the Senate. Annual reports will include information on the federal government's progress relative to FEPA.

Confidential information processing protection

Perhaps the most crucial part of Title III is the requirements for protecting sensitive information. Congress found that there was no single method for collecting data, and as a result, the public's trust declined. During the Committee's investigation, the group found that different agencies used different techniques for protecting public information. Congress recognized that defending personally identifiable information (PII) serves public and societal interests. If the public distrusts the federal government with their data, the public's distrust would negatively affect the accuracy and completeness of any resulting statistical analysis.

FEPA distinguishes two types of data uses: data collected for "statistical" and "non-statistical" reasons. Statistical use refers to data that the federal government uses for analytical purposes as part of an analytic inquiry. Non-statistical use refers to evidence the government uses for purposes other than statistical activities and can be shared among agencies but may or may not be shareable outside the agency. Data collected for non-statistical purposes can be shared more broadly and has fewer restrictions.

Title III also places restrictions on how the government releases another class of data, namely personally identifiable information (PII). Agencies may disclose PII only with the consent of the respondent and just for statistical purposes. The law requires agency head approval for the release, and the releasing agency handles confirming there are no other restrictions to prohibit the agency from releasing the PII. For example, agencies must ensure that there are no other legal restrictions on a release, like a private contractor statutory limitation.

To help drive home the seriousness of protecting confidential data, FEPA assigns strict fines for nonconformance. Anyone who willfully discloses the data to someone who is not entitled to receive it is guilty of a Class E felony and imprisoned for not more than five years or fined not more than $250,000, or both.

Statistical efficiency

In today's fast-paced world, businesses, consumers, investors, and others are using data to inform their decisions. As part of their research, the Committee discovered that federal agencies met legal constraints that prevented federal agencies from sharing data and increasing the efficiency and efficacy of official statistical inquiries. At the same time, survey respondents began questioning whether the government could protect their personal information.

It became clear that the quality of research directly depended on the willingness of respondents to answer statistical surveys honestly. The Committee also recognized that lowering the reporting burdens on federal agencies would lead to more correct depictions of the economy and its health. So, for instance, if the Bureau of the Census (USCB), the Bureau of Economic Analysis, and the Bureau of Labor Statistics (BLS) share data more effectively, the federal government should have a deeper understanding of American businesses and how the landscape was changing. Also, if federal agencies used uniform data standards when categorizing industries, all agencies could drill down to find and resolve specific industry problems related to their agencies. They could adjust for new businesses entering and exiting the national economy and to any irregularities that arise.

Furthermore, Title III expands the amount of data each agency can collect and analyze. It also extends the number of industry classifications from 135 to over 800, supplying the government more granularity when reviewing the state of the economy.

Designated statistical agencies

The title's goal is to increase the government's overall understanding of the US economy, especially in areas reflecting the nation's most important economic indicators, like income and product accounts. Accordingly, the law improves the semantic and syntactic similarity and accuracy of the federal economic statistics that these agencies produce. Title III explicitly authorizes the sharing of business data among the Bureau of the Census (USCB), the Bureau of Economic Analysis (BEA), and the Bureau of Labor Statistics (BLS) for statistical purposes to reduce paperwork burdens on businesses. These three are Designated Statistical Agencies (DSAs).

DSAs are doing a lot of the heavy lifting under FEPA. These agencies, or divisions of agencies, produce and disseminate relevant and timely statistical information. Title III charges these agencies with conducting credible and correct statistical inquiries and running objectively. Because FSAs hold the public's data, these agencies are the last line of defense for protecting confidential information and making sure that data is used for statistical purposes only. Following OMB's guidance, each DSA will then set up policies, best practices, and other procedures to conduct their work, and each agency head will enable and support their respective organization to produce evidence for policymakers.

While DSAs are being held accountable for what you would expect—the elimination of duplicate data and improvement of data quality and cost control, they are also responsible for protecting the confidentiality of collected PII. Specifically, DSAs must ensure that leadership, staff, and agents, such as academics and contractors, are aware of the importance of keeping confidential information under tight control. In this case, awareness applies to any agencies that use confidential information. DSAs ensure organizations that are given access and use the sensitive data fully understand their legal obligation to protect PII. Protections help both document business processes as well as develop physical and electronic security for safeguarding confidential data. Security procedures also include managing an audit log of everyone who accesses sensitive data.

When DSAs share data, they must conform to new sharing requirements and written agreements reflecting binding terms. Only officers, staff, and agents who are parties to the data-sharing agreements are allowed access to the data.

Access to data for evidence

Title III presumes that DSAs have access to data to support analytical inquiries, and other federal agencies are compelled to make a copy of their data available upon request. The title also requires that DSAs promptly respond to data requests and provide requestors with specific statutes that prohibit a DSA from sharing their data with requestors. Title III requires agencies to set up and follow regular and transparent processes to conduct interagency data exchanges.

Expanding secure access to CIPSEA data assets

Not all federally collected data will be right for public access, however. Some data has sensitive governmental information and is suitable only for interagency sharing. The Confidential Information Protection and Statistical Efficiency Act of 2002 (CIPSEA) was passed to handle these situations. This law supplies strong confidentiality protections for statistical information collecting sponsored or conducted by Federal agencies.

Under FEPA, confidential information will be more specifically defined. Federal agencies will be needed to produce a system to categorize the relative sensitivity and the corresponding level of accessibility for each data asset. The categorization system includes shared sensitivity levels, criteria for assigning sensitivity levels, rules for producing a lesser sensitive version of a data asset, and standards to improve access by redacting specific information. Title III also requires FSAs to perform a risk assessment for any data asset that the government intends to release to the public. FSAs must ensure that the evaluation is easy to understand and available on the national data catalog. Additionally, FSAs must publish their standards and procedures on the national data catalog as well.

Applying to access data assets for developing evidence

Title III also directs OMB to develop a process through which the Congressional Budget Office (CBO), as well as state, local, and tribal government researchers, or other individuals, can apply for access to data assets covered under this new law. The law explicitly requires OMB to ensure that FSAs produce *identical* processes, using a standard application form and criteria, and timeframes for turnaround, appeals, and standards. Title III also requires OMB to guide FSAs to develop the same processes in coordination with public and private stakeholders.

Analysis

These thoughts were offered in the immediate passing of the legislation. The following represents our best guess as to what FEPA means for both government and the private sector. We conclude by specifically mentioning eight areas that we feel require further analysis and welcome the ensuing discussion.

What does this mean?

Better data sharing among designated groups have a variety of benefits, not the least of which is less spending by government agencies to produce the same data—a big win for taxpayers. The long-term impacts of this new law are difficult to measure and will be heavily dependent on the law's practical implementation. However, what is clear is that we now have a law on the books and an opportunity to track any resulting issues and measure their relative impact going forward. The effect will be that agencies must plan in writing which open data will be used by specified models to produce named outputs. The effect is to impose objective professionalism on the federal government's decision-making process and will be felt throughout the US economy. Here are some potential effects that the authors have already showed:

- **Overall impact potential.** The federal government accounts for 33% of our national economy and has a considerable data asset collection. The immediate effect will be on organizations interacting with the federal government who stand to receive help from the resulting improved standardization. There will be a significant impact at other levels outside government, namely on business, academia, and other organizations. What sort of consequences the new legislation creates and how those impacts affect different groups is not readily apparent beyond a significant increase in the maturity of the involved data practices.

- **Greater data sharing examples.** The new legislation supplies specific authority to DSAs to share data, allowing those agencies to access each other's data. The government's goal is to achieve higher interoperability among the DSAs and expand the practice of using uniform confidentiality protections by respective FSAs. The federal government can create more interoperability only through detailed and carefully controlled interoperation. The success of this effort can be used as a model to apply throughout other parts of the federal government.

- **Knowledge worker value.** Presently, the federal government has trouble paying market rates for data expertise. As the federal government shifts to using data for more decision-making, there are opportunities for data personnel to receive higher compensation at rates comparable to industry rates. However, with an equal increase in demand for these skills, the government may still fall yet farther behind and unable to compete for scarce resources in the market.

- **Data as a gateway.** To be useful across agencies, the federal government must adopt a unifying measurement framework. If the government can better manage its data, many other things become more comfortable, including decision making, process design, and standards. According to The Center for Data Innovation, open data has enormous value for businesses, journalists, academics, civil society groups, and even other government agencies. These organizations use the vast supply of data the federal government makes freely available in open formats online to develop innovative products and services, set up critical business decisions, conduct research, and ensure accountability and oversight in government. (Riley, 2019).

- **Uniform confidentiality approach.** When all agencies are sharing data in the same way, individuals and organizations are more likely to trust their information is protected and more likely to share information. When this happens, this directly leads to cost reduction. Greater access to data between agencies means agencies do not have to spend money to recreate data they need or buy data from third-party sources (Bean, 2018). As with unifying measurements, it is unclear whether agencies will be able to adopt the same confidentiality rules fully, or whether differing legal requirements will limit the unification of approaches.

- **State government impacts.** State and local governments use federal data whenever they must through federal grants. As federal agencies change their approach to data and its usage, there is potential for state and local governments to do the same.

- **Remainder impacts.** Though not explicitly set up by the statute, we have seen instances with earlier federal data mandates where other "knock on" effects can occur, including:

  o Continued focus in the financial and other historically numbers-driven industries.
  o Corresponding increases in training and other immersion opportunities for federal employees should result.
  o The potential for research communities to focus more on the use of data instead of just new results.
  o Added experiences, benchmarks, and best practices to compare against the private sector.
  o Governments uncover more public-private partnership opportunities.
  o Improved efficiencies and effectiveness afford the government greater leverage.

Potential challenges and unanswered questions

As data advocates, we believe more power over data is better. The fact that FEPA was passed so quickly compared to other federal data statutes is exciting. However, it is important to understand and track the impacts so that the government can make prompt measured adjustments, and the federal government can continue to lead the way for state and local governments to drive more data usage in their constituencies.

Greater data availability helps all citizens and American businesses, but it is not without consequences. Responsible rollout and management are critical at this exciting juncture. While the statutory changes show promise in many areas, our team still sees concern and open questions in some key areas:

1. **Separation of duties.** For the first time, the legislation shows a clear separation of duties between the CDO and CIO. No longer is data a byproduct of technology and the responsibility of the CIO. Instead, data is the business, and how organizations use and share data are decisions that the business owns. More work needs to be done to ensure that technology does not eclipse these ideals.

2. **The potential for creation of economic imbalances.** Information is power, or, to put it

more finely, disproportionate access to information is power. While the new law gives the public greater access to massive amounts of government data, the ability to process and make sense of all that data will not be equally available to all citizens.

3. **Taxpayers are the product.** Based on some initial research, large companies, academia, and watchdog organizations are the beneficiaries of FEPA. These organizations stand for a tiny part of the wider public. On the other hand, companies like Experian, Equifax, Transunion, Facebook, and a host of other large companies have strong abilities to process and monetize government data to their advantage. Right now, they already collect a massive amount of data from citizens—where data is the product they sell to other companies. With the passage of FEPA, all companies will also have access to government data, which may either enrich the company's 'products' currently available with taxpayer data or make these products less valuable since the government will make the data available for free.

4. **International trade imbalance.** Foreign corporations would also have access to data available under FEPA. That may allow them the opportunity to take advantage of data describing American citizens and disadvantage US companies on the world stage. Few countries have open data

programs that are as sweeping as the United States. It is not clear whether the added data availability created by FEPA will inspire other countries to do the same.

5. **Implementing standards.** FEPA requires OMB to set up rules about the marking and handling of federal data. President Obama signed Executive Order 13556 in 2010 that requires federal agencies to mark data using standardized marks and tags to distinguish data that the federal government considers sensitive and worthy of control. There is a significant cost associated with complying with any standard. It is still unclear how these standards interact with one another and under what conditions.

6. **Unreasonable performance standards.** Industry consumes federal data and incorporates that data into products and services. As demand for industry services continues to grow, the industry is appealing to customers with various claims— performance, quality, relevance, etc. Because the federal government is the originator of that industry data, the government inherits costs associated with improved data timeliness without its knowledge or consent. So, while the law has not funded this effort, the industry's needs may influence the government's hand in the future.

7. **No added spending, but no payoff either.** Businesses sell data for a profit. Governments charge taxes and tariffs on products and services, which is then used for national purposes. If data has value, why can the government not glean more revenue for it? By freely releasing other data under FEPA, the government may be devaluing it to the detriment of the American taxpayer.

8. **Lack of objective criteria for personnel.** What constitutes a qualified CDO is ambiguous? Depending on the bent of any agency, CDOs could come in all shapes and forms. The legislation specifies:

   (b) QUALIFICATIONS.—The Chief Data Officer of an agency shall be designated on the basis of demonstrated training and experience in data management, governance (including creation, application, and maintenance of data standards), collection, analysis, protection, use, and dissemination, including with respect to any statistical and related techniques to protect and de-identify confidential data.

How these issues translate into a formalized credentialing system is still to be seen. Were we discussing a traditional and formalized profession like dentistry, we would have shared expectations. However, because CDOs are new and academia has not designed an underlying educational curriculum, those shared expectations do not exist.

CHAPTER 12

What Some States are Doing

"If we have data, let's look at data. If all we have are opinions, let's go with mine."

— Jim Barksdale, former Netscape CEO

Highlighting other people's work is always a tricky topic. On the one hand, we want to name organizations and efforts that are worthy of attention, and plenty are worth highlighting. However, no matter how many we recognize and no matter how we describe them, we are going to leave something off the list that someone else believes should be included. We intend to showcase a few examples where public sector organizations are doing hard and vital data management work.

Why them? Two simple reasons: first, many of us come from public sector data work and know how challenging it can be, and, second, if a government can make it work, then what excuse do any of the rest of us have? If you believe the work you are doing in your organization calls for such accolades, please email us.

State of Arkansas: Data inventory

After the State of Arkansas appointed its first CDO, early discussions with agency leadership highlighted a huge gap in the data scenery of the state. Not all state departments kept an inventory of data assets. Despite pressure to do more with data, the CDO concluded the state was not ready to conduct advanced data analytics without first understanding what data the state kept. The CDO recognized the state needed to understand crucial information about its data holdings to meet legal requirements. For example, Arkansas needs to know who owns and stewards a data asset. The state needs to know the contact information for each steward, and the state needs to know the sharing requirements for each data asset. Because the State of Arkansas wished for a state data center consolidation as well as a shared services transformation, the CDO prioritized developing a central repository of the state's high-value data assets.

State of Indiana: Data analytics

The Indiana Management Performance Hub (MPH) set out to change the culture of how state agencies worked together and how they interacted with external partners. MPH combined a collaborative and innovative approach with industry-leading technical innovation to help data-driven decision making and data-informed policy making.

As part of this work, the MPH set up several goals for itself.

- Become the highest performing state government using data-driven decision making.

- Provide world-class data science and analytics capabilities to partners to help inform and solve policy challenges.

- Provide a platform to be the data hub for Indiana governments and citizens to foster transparency and problem-solving.

- Provide Hoosiers with a return on investment in MPH by developing new revenue streams through the leveraging of the MPH platform.

- Provide the backbone to help make Indiana become a national leader in data analytics and science and helping foster economic development in Indiana.

In 2017, the *Indiana Open Data Act* formally codified the MPH as a standalone state agency with the power to collect, analyze, and exchange data across state agencies. MPH is revolutionizing the way these agencies, non-governmental partners, and citizens access and visualize critical data that can help drive data-informed decision making and data-driven policymaking.

State of Michigan: Executive charter

Not unlike many governments, the customers of the State of Michigan must interact with multiple programs to receive services and conduct business. State programs often function as autonomous providers of services, with the integrated coordination of customer service being the exception rather than the rule. This model resulted in approximately 10 million customers coordinating services and conducting business with dozens of state programs. Recognizing this problem, Governor Rick Snyder challenged the state to reinvent itself by improving data sharing across all executive branch agencies. The Governor noted that data and information are valued assets that require effective and secure management to enhance services to citizens. According to Governor Snyder, this can only be done by setting up an Enterprise Information Management (EIM) program.

To that end, Governor Snyder signed Executive Order (EO) 2016-24 in December 2016. The EO gives the Department of Technology, Management, and Budget (DTMB) primary responsibility for the implementation of an EIM program and names the projects and goals of the program. The EO also requires the creation of an EIM steering committee. It further requires that each state department set up an information management governance board and appoint a chief data steward. Projects and goals of the EIM must include the establishment of a single internet sign-on, improved quality of data and service delivery, and cross-agency data sharing.

State of Texas: Information sharing

A key enabler for Texas to be able to respond so quickly to evolving requirements was through its ability to share data across organizational boundaries. To achieve this, the State of Texas created a standard data sharing agreement that reduced barriers to inter-agency data exchange. By documenting required legal components up-front, program areas were able to execute data sharing more efficiently and with less variation across the controlling documentation. The executive directors of the Health and Human Services Commission, the Texas Department of Public Safety, the Texas Workforce Commission, and the Department of Information Resources have already signed and implemented the agreement.

Key takeaways

- **Study the other sector.** Both private and public CDOs face similar challenges, but they also face many common, noteworthy obstacles.

- **Think in broad terms.** Organizational differences also supply an opportunity to structure or shift strategies to accommodate the differences.

- **Not every solution must come from you.** There are simply too many differences and challenges for one person or one team to solve! Utilize organizational resources, including people in your organization— and across other organizations—to adapt to these challenges and thrive.

- **Not all differences are unique.** Look for solutions in other sectors and other industries as well. Often, modifications of other proven solutions can hold the key to success within your organization and your parameters.

Public References

The following is a list of laws and executive orders that governments have enacted to help set up and institutionalize the chief data officer role.

1. State of Arkansas (2016) House Bill 1793: To Create the Chief Data Officer and Chief Privacy Officer (pp 1—6)

Intent: To create a panel on data transparency, to create the position the chief data officer and chief privacy officer within the Department of Information Systems.

2. State of California (2017, November 4) AB-1215: California Open Data Standard

Intent: CDO, who shall be appointed by, and serve at the pleasure of, the Governor. The Chief Data Officer shall report to the Secretary of Government Operations, create an inventory of all available public data in the state, and establish an internet web portal at data.ca.gov.

3. State of Colorado (2014) 8 CCR 1501-7: Rule in Support of Centralized IT Management and Creation of Enterprise Architecture Office and Data Management Program, 1—4

Intent: To use data and information as enterprise assets and to establish standards and processes to enable more agile solutions and government services.

4. State of Colorado (2009) Colorado Revised Statutes Title 24 Government State § 24-375-703 Government data advisory Board—Created—Duties—Repeal, 1—12

Intent: To advise the CIO regarding the ongoing development, maintenance, and implementation of the interdepartmental data protocol; to advise the CIO concerning best practices in sharing and protecting data in state government; and to recommend to the CIO rules and procedures that a state agency shall follow in requesting, or responding to a request for, data from another state agency, including but not limited to strategies for enforcing said rules.

5. State of Indiana (2018) Indiana Code Title 4 State Offices and Administration § 4-3-26-10, 1—4

Intent: To establish the Indiana Management Performance Hub (MPH) and establish the role of the Indiana CDO, who will serve as the executive head of the MPH, advise executive state agencies and political subdivisions regarding state best practices concerning the creation and maintenance of data, and coordinate data analytics and transparency master planning for the executive state agencies and provide leadership regarding state data analytics and transparency.

6. State of Michigan (2016) Executive Order No 2016-24: Enterprise Information Management, 1—7

Intent: To set up a governance structure to guide the design, development, and implementation of a statewide-integrated criminal justice environment that would enable automated information sharing in a generic format between state, local, and federal criminal justice agencies.

7. State of Michigan (2013) Executive Order No 2013-1: Data and Information Sharing, Management and Governance, 1—2

Intent: To set up a state-wide data sharing body which makes rules about the use of state data.

8. State of New Jersey (2018) 52 18A-2344 Chief Data Officer: Appointment, Authority, Responsibilities; Rules, Regulations, 1—1

Intent: To set up within the state a CDO position. Statute names the authorities and responsibilities for the role.

9. State of New Jersey (2018) 52 18A-2345: Provision of Information by Agency, 1—1

Intent: Requires that state agencies supply datasets to the CDO in a prescribed format.

10. State of North Carolina (2018) North Carolina General Statutes Chapter 143B Executive Organization Act of 1973 § 143B-1385: Government Data Analytics Center, 1—598

Intent: To set up the process of collecting, organizing, sharing, and analyzing data through integrated data management, reporting, visualization, and advanced analytics to discover patterns and other useful information that will allow policymakers and state officials to make more informed decisions.

11. State of Texas (2015) HB 1912 Subchapter B, Chapter 2054, Government Code, is amended by adding Section 20540286

Intent: Relating to employment of a statewide data coordinator in the Department of Information Resources.

12. State of Texas (2015) SB 1844 Subtitle B, Title 10, Government Code, is amended by adding Chapter 2060

Intent: Relating to the establishment and functions of the Interagency Data Transparency Commission. The commission is created to study and review the current public data structure, classification, sharing, and reporting protocols for state agencies.

13. State of Vermont (2018) 3 App VSA Ch 22, § 7: Creation of the Agency of Digital Services, 1—3

Intent: To set up the Division of Data Management within the Agency of Digital Services (ADS).

14. US federal government (2018) Federal Evidence-Based Policy Act

Intent: To set up evidence-based policy decision, open data program, chief data officers, and access to data for evidence.

References

Aiken, P, & Billings, J (2013) *Monetizing Data Management: Finding the Value in Your Organization's Most Important Asset.* Basking Ridge, NJ: Technics Publications, LLC.

Aiken, P, & Gorman, M (2014) "The case for the chief data officer." *Harvard Business Review*, 1-90.

Aiken, P, & Harbour, T (2017) *Data Strategy and the Enterprise Data Executive: Ensuring that Business and IT are in Synch in the Post-Big Data Era* (pp 1-248).

Andersen, B, & Fagerhaug, T (2015) *Root Cause Analysis: Simplified Tools and Techniques*, 1-169.

Anthony, S D (2018) What do you really mean by Business "Transformation?" 1-4.

Ash Center (2019) Who are America's city chief data officers? datasmart.ash.harvard.edu/news/article/data-leadership-at-the-executive-level-761.

Beeson, J (2018). Five questions every leader should ask about organizational design, Harvard Business Review, 1-6.

Boris. (2019, February 04). What makes storytelling so effective for learning? Retrieved April 08, 2020, from https://s.hbr.org/377kFug.

Bragg M. (2018). *GAAP Guidebook*. Centennial, CO: AccountingTools.

Brown, B, Court, D, & Willmott, P (2013) Can your c-suite handle big data? Harvard Business Review, 1-5.

Buytendijk, F, & Oestreich, T W (2017) *Organizing for Big Data through Better Process and Governance* (pp 1-13).

Cameron, K S, & Quinn, R E (2008) *Diagnosing and Changing Organizational Culture* (pp 1-259) John Wiley & Sons, Inc.

Carnegie Mellon University (2014) Data Management Maturity Model v10 (pp 1-248).

Cartwright, T, & Baldwin, D (2014) *Communicating your Vision* (pp 1-35).

Carande, C, Lipinski, P, & Gusher, T (2017) How to integrate data and analytics into every art of your organization, Harvard Business Review, (pp 1-5).

Covert, A., & Fenton, N. (2014). *How to Make Sense of any Mess*. Abby Covert.

Cox, I, Weldon, L, & Sinha, M (2017) The case for change: Why digital business needs a new approach to strategy, 1-8.

DalleMule, L, & Davenport, T H (2017) What's your data strategy? Harvard Business Review, (pp 1-11).

DeCarlo, S, & VanderMey, A (2019) The 14 longest serving CEOs of the fortune 500, Fortune, 1-5.

Desjardins, J (2018) The rise of the chief data officer (CDO), Retrieved August 24, 2018, from https://bit.ly/2XHiD0F.

Eisenhower, D. (1950), Volume XI: Columbia University, Editor Louis Galambos et al, Letter from: Dwight Eisenhower, Letter to: Hamilton Fish Armstrong, Date: December 31, 1950, Start Page 1516, Quote Page 1516, Johns Hopkins University Press, Baltimore, Maryland.

Evernden, R., & Evernden, E. (2011). *Information First: Integrating Knowledge and Information Architecture for Business Advantage*. London: Routledge.

Faria, M (2015) Chief Data Officers should Align Authority and Responsibility to Succeed (pp 1-9).

Forrester, E. C., Buteau, B. L., & Shrum, S. (2011). *CMMI for Services: Guidelines for Superior Service* (Second Edition, pp. 1-790). Pearson Education, Inc.

French, W L, & Bell, C (2001) *Organization Development: Behavioral Science Interventions for Organization Improvement*, Upper Saddle River, NJ: Prentice Hall

Geddes, M (2016) *Making Public Private Partnerships Work*, (pp 1-151).

George, J M, & Jones, G R (2008) *Understanding and Managing Organizational Behavior* (pp 1-694).

General Services Administration Federal Acquisition Regulation (Vol 1, pp 1-2013).

Government Technology (2015) Colorado names new chief data officer, Retrieved August 24, 2018, from https://bit.ly/2AJP1qG.

Griffith, T (2018) Are we asking too much of our CIOs? Harvard Business Review, 1-4.

Griffith, T (2017) Just adding a chief data officer isn't enough, (pp 1-4).

Hagerty, J (2015) *Developing Buy-in for Change*, 1-19.

Harvey, C R, & Liu, Y (2014) *Evaluating Trading Strategies*, 1-11.

Helms, M (2018) *Encyclopedia of Management*, 6th Edition, 1-6.

Hitt, M A, Colella, A, & Miller, C (2014) *Organizational Behavior*. Wiley Global Education.

Holzner, M, & Charbonneau, E (2008) *Public Management & Administration Illustrated*, 1-135.

Horodyski, J (2011) *Digital Asset Management* (DAM), (pp 1-6).

Hubbard W. (2010). How to measure anything: Finding the value of "intangibles" in business. Chichester, West Sussex: John Wiley & Sons.

Information Security Oversight Office (ISOO) (2018) 32 CFR 2002: Controlled unclassified information (CUI), 1-25.

Kambil, A (2018) Four types of executive sponsorship to catalyze change. The Wall Street Journal, 1-7

Kass, E M (2017) *Companies will soon be valued by their data assets.*

Kelley, J (2018) *How to Manage your Boss*, 1-3.

Kendle, N (2013) *The Data Management Organization: Key to Effective Data Management*, 1-43.

Kotter, J P (1978) *Organizational Dynamics: Diagnosis and Intervention Reading*, MAMA: Addison-Wesley.

Kotter, J P (1995) Leading change: Why transformation efforts fail. Harvard Business Review, 1-3 .

Ladley, J (2010) *Making Enterprise Information Management (EIM) Work for Business: A Guide to Understanding Information as an Asset*. Elsevier Inc.

Laney, D B (2018) Infonomics: *How to Monetize, Manage, and Measure Information as an Asset for Competitive Advantage* New York, NY: Bibliomotion, Inc.

Lant, J. L. (1993). *No More Cold Calls: The Complete Guide to Generating, and Closing, all the Prospects you need to become a Multi-millionaire by Selling your Service.* Cambridge, MA: JLA Publications.

Lavigna, R (2014, November 28) Why government workers are harder to motivate. Harvard Business Review, 1-6.

Lavoie, B F (2014) The open archival information system (OAIS) reference model: Introductory guide (2nd Edition) (pp 1-37) Digital Preservation Coalition.

LeBoeuf, M. (1989). *The Greatest Management Principle in the World*. New York: Berkley Books.

Letzter, R (2019) Tons of pressurized oxygen could be hiding out in earth's molten iron core, 1-3.

Lippitt, M (2003) *Leading Complex Change Enterprise Management*, LTD.

Logan, D, White, A, & Bugajski, J (2015) *The Chief Data Officer's First 100 Days* (pp 1-17).

Logan, D, Dayley, A, & Childs, S (2016) *Data Governance Best Practice: Adopt a Use Case Approach* 1-9.

Luscher, L, & Lewis, M (2008) *Organizational Change and Managerial Sensemaking: Working Through Paradox* (Vol 52). Academy of Management Journal.

Mayer, D, & Greenberg, H M (2018) *What Makes a Good Salesman*, 1-16.

McGilvray, D (2008) *Executing Data Quality Projects* (pp 1-332) Morgan Kaufmann.

McPherson, K, & Wright, B (2018) Gone to Texas: Migration, 1-7.

Meier, K, & O'Toole, L (2011) Comparing Public and Private Management: Theoretical Expectations Journal of Public Administration Research and Theory: J-PART, 21, 1283-1299.

Morgan, T D (2010) *The Vanishing American Lawyer* (pp 1-260).

Myler, L (2013) Strategy 101: It is all about alignment, Retrieved April 02, 2019, from https://bit.ly/3hazNf9.

National Archives (2018) National archives history, Retrieved March 12, 2019, from https://wwwarchivesgov/about/history.

Nautin, T (2013) *The Aligned Organization*, 1-7.

Project Management Institute (PMI) (2013) *A Guide to the Project Management Body of Knowledge (PMBOK Guide).*

Rainey, H G (2013) *Understanding and Managing Public Organizations* (pp 1-594).

Redmen, T (2017) Steele, J (2015) *Understanding the Chief Data Officer* (pp 1-4).

Rosenfeld, A R (2012) In lawyer-client relationship, who makes the decisions? Retrieved August 8, 2018, from https://newenglandinhousecom/2012/07/16/in-lawyer-client-relationship-who-makes-the-decisions/.

Russom, P (2008) *Data Governance Strategies: Helping your Organization Comply, Transform, and Integrate* (pp 1-32).

Sampson, A (2012) *Do not be Afraid to Complain about your Lawyer says Legal Ombudsman.*

Sapp, C E, Brabham, D, Antelmi, J, et al (2018) *2019 Planning Guide for Data and Analytics.*

Samuels, M. (2019). What is a chief data officer? Everything you must know about the CDO role, Retrieved May 11, 2019, from https://zd.net/3eYULvl.

Satterfield, A (2015) *The Six Dimensions of EHDI Data Quality Assessment*, 1-4.

Schaeffer, L D, Schultz, A M, & Salerno, J A (2009) *HHS in the 21st Century: Charting a New Course for a Healthier America.* Washington, DC: National Academies Press.

Senge, P M (2018) *The Fifth Discipline: The Art & Practice of the Learning Organization.*

The Standish Group International, Inc. (2016). CHAOS report 2016, Retrieved October 04, 2019, from https://www.standishgroup.com/outline.

Stastna, K. (2012). What are crown corporations and why do they exist? | CBC News. Retrieved May 11, 2019, from https://bit.ly/2MzPm1P.

Steele, J (2015) *Understanding the Chief Data Officer* (pp 1-26).

Taylor, D. (1997). *The Healing Power of Stories: Creating Yourself through the Stories of your Life.* Alexandria, N.S.W.: Millennium Books.

Teixeira, R (2008) Red, blue, and purple America: The future of election demographics, 1-285.

Texas Demographic Center (2017) Texas migration, 1-16.

Tracy, B (2013) The four factors of motivation, Retrieved August 8, 2018, from https://bit.ly/2UidTMQ.

Treasury Board of Canada Secretariat. (2019). Guidance for crown corporations, Retrieved May 11, 2019, from https://bit.ly/37b6JiS.

U.S. Census Bureau (2014) Governing calculations of US census bureau 2014 annual survey of public employment & payroll data.

U.S. Small Business Administration (SBA). (2019). Firm size sata I The U.S. small business administration, Retrieved May 12, 2019, from https://www.sba.gov/advocacy/firm-size-data.

Vogel, D (1990) 'Kill the lawyers,' A line misinterpreted, Retrieved March 27, 2019, from https://nyti.ms/2Y9VjYH.

Wachs, H L (2015) Improving data governance with effective data discovery, 1-16.

Westervelt, A (2018) Why business transformation fails and how to ensure it doesn't Forbes, 1-5.

Worley, C G, & Feyerherm, A E (2003) Reflections on the future of organization development The Journal of Applied Behavioral Science, 39(1), 97-115 doi:101177/0021886303039001005.

Zaidi, E, De Simoni, G, Edjlali, R, & Duncan, A D (2018) *Data Catalogs are the New Black in Data Management and Analytics*, 1-16.

Zimmermann, K (2017) What is culture? Retrieved March 13, 2019, from https://bit.ly/2Un8JPX.

Index

Made in the USA
Middletown, DE
13 July 2020